D1081700

BIBLE AND LITERATURE
SERIES

Editor
David M. Gunn

IMAGES OF MAN AND GOD

Old Testament Short Stories
in Literary Focus

Editor
BURKE O. LONG

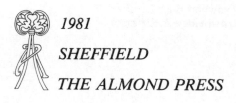

1981

SHEFFIELD

THE ALMOND PRESS

Copyright © 1981 The Almond Press

British Library Cataloguing in Publication Data:

Images of man and God. - (Bible and literature
   series, ISSN 0260-4493; 1)
   1. Bible as literature   2. Bible. O.T. -
   Criticism, interpretation, etc.
   I. Long, Burke O.   II. Series
   221.6   BS535

   ISBN 0-907459-00-5
   ISBN 0-907459-01-3 Pbk

Published by
The Almond Press
P.O. Box 208
Sheffield S10 5DW
England

Text-edited on a
Wang Word Processor
in Madeleine PS typestyle

Printed in Great Britain
by Redwood Burn Limited
Trowbridge & Esher
1981

CONTENTS

CONTRIBUTORS

James Crenshaw

Professor of Old Testament
Vanderbilt University

David Gunn

Lecturer in Biblical Studies
The University of Sheffield

Burke Long

Professor of Religion
Bowdoin College

Errol McGuire

Assistant Professsor of Religion
    and Literature
Virginia Polytechnic Institute
    and State University

James Nohrnberg

Professor of English
The University of Virginia

John Vickery

Professor of English
The University of California,
    Riverside

PREFACE

I T may appear anachronistic to speak of short story in the Old Testament - not because people invented brief story-telling only after Biblical times, for they obviously did not. But anachronistic in the sense that, in conventional language, the term "short story" first calls to mind modern examples. We generally think of artfully constructed fiction, a tightly unified narrative work associated with authors of the nineteenth and twentieth centuries, such as Scott, Hawthorne, or Chekhov.

I have used "short story" in the title of this book deliberately to suggest a focus upon brief, self-contained narratives, treated as if they were works of fiction. The contributors to this volume do not deny what may be history in the stories they write about. Nor do they dismiss or ignore established results of historical scholarship. Indeed, some of them clearly depend upon certain of these results.[1]

Rather they seek together to lay aside or de-emphasize the more usual philological and historical concerns so as to highlight the Old Testament as story, that is as a rich, human world created in the meeting of author and reader. They attempt to draw out something of the deep emotional power of these stories, a power which has never been merely seated in intellectual formulation of doctrine, or in historical "realia", or in shifting theories of criticism. The somewhat dated words of John Cowper Powys are worth repeating:

> The power of the Bible does not lie in its doctrine, does not lie in its spirituality, does not even lie in its righteousness. It lies in its supreme emotional contradictions, each carried to its uttermost extreme, and each representing, finally and for all time, some unchanging aspect of human life upon earth.[2]

Or again, in the words of Reynolds Price, Southerner, novelist, one drawn to the Bible for deeply humanistic, cultural, yet religious reasons:

> The root of story sprang from need - need for
> companionship and consolation by a creature as
> vulnerable, four million years ago as now, as any
> protozoan in a warm brown swamp. The need is not for
> the total consolation of narcotic fantasy - our own will
> performed in airless triumph - but for credible news
> that our lives proceed in order toward a pattern....We
> crave nothing less than perfect story; and while we
> chatter or listen all our lives in a din of craving - jokes,
> anecdotes, novels, dreams, films, plays, songs, half the
> words of our days - we are satisfied only by the one
> short tale we feel to be true: History is the will of a
> just god who knows us.[3]

The essays in this volume do not offer theology, though
they suggest spirituality; they do not serve up history, nicely
turned out on platters of polished erudition, though they may
illuminate history. The authors look to their own response to
the worlds created by story, and seek to make clear - as in a
mirror - the visions of human and religious truth found there.
As readers, we are made to glimpse their imaginings - the
critic's and the storyteller's - so as to see all the more some
pattern and order, sense and metaphor, evocative symbol in
our own lives.

The contributors espouse no particular critical theories,
though one may find hints of indebtedness here and there.
Nor do they discuss theory.[4] They engage in criticism.
Which is to say that they implicitly hold that the best and
richest comment grows out of close reading of a text. Our
intent is that you the reader of this volume might see anew,
with freshened insight and quickened response.[5]

Burke O. Long
Bowdoin College

Chapter One

THE JOSEPH STORY: A TALE OF SON AND FATHER

Errol M. McGuire

THe Joseph story, the extended narrative which concludes the Book of Genesis, is among the most carefully composed, imaginatively provocative, and structurally unified, short works in the Bible. As with the remainder of the canonical materials, of course, this narrative has long posed intriguing textual, source, and historical critical problems for the scholar's consideration. But as Paul Ricoeur has recently helped us to understand, there is an equally important world which any great story evokes and creates, one which lies, as it were, "in front of" the text, that "world" which the story as literature generates within our imaginations, or in that space between our internal expectations and the external presentation within the story's house of images. There, in the imagination - where all stories truly live - the well-wrought tale gives us both tools and incentive to see our common, ordinary world with fresh, even visionary, eyes; to recognize and sense that reality is a far more marvelous and complex thing than perhaps we had once earlier conceived, and ultimately to enjoy that new fullness of vision and feeling. In literature we are also sometimes compelled to re-examine our values and experiences in ways that pure reason, discursive argument, or various responses to law alone could never cause us to do. This is an advantage which fiction nearly always maintains over abstract moral or social philosophy; it allows us to imagine fully what it might really feel like to hold a given position in a given world.

None of this will surprise the person who knows how exciting many of the Old Testament stories can be for children. Isaac Bashevis Singer, in accepting his recent Nobel Prize for literature, noted that the unflagging attention of children is among the best possible signs of excellence in literature. Children know a good tale when they hear one. The actual number of rhetorical impacts which a given story may have upon an audience can, of course, be large indeed. But of the crucial importance of the place and function of story (or myth) in culture there can no long be any doubt. Mircea Eliade, has argued, for example, that story-telling is one of our indispensable links - particularly in contemporary society - with our ancient and primal roots, and with the deep sources of sacrality which have been so obscured by secularity and its distorting one-dimensinal versions of experience. We need stories, quite literally, in order to survive; they enable us, Eliade asserts, to "demystify" the increasingly profane world and, by indirection, to bring it round to its authentic sacred centers. The excesssive contemporary devotion to rationality and to the structures of secular value must be balanced, he goes on to contend, with the freedom and spontaneity of the imagination, particularly as expressed in the "play" offered by narrative and the poetic realm in general.[1]

A story as powerful and appealing as the one I want to speak about here deserves to be taken with full seriousness as the literature it actually is, literature which has helped to shape the mental worlds of many western cultures, Jewish and Christian. My intention here, therefore, is to comment on this story in Genesis as a product of the ancient literary imagination and to clarify how it functions as a piece of literature in its own right. As much as possible, I want to regard this tale as if it were the creation of single authorial presence - not only acknowledge its rhetorical effectiveness as a poetic whole, but to assess and portray more adequately its distinctive literary and mythic features.

I

The Joseph story begins after the conclusion of a loose collection of diverse narrative material depicting the life of Jacob and a genealogical survey of Esau's family. The story is announced as the history of Jacob's family, but clearly it remains largely Joseph's own story throughout, in spite of the intrusion of the account of Judah and Tamar (chapter 38) and the concluding blessings of Jacob on his children (chapter 49). As the tale opens, the young teenage hero is enjoying a special position of prestige in the household of his father. This position, due to his being the firstborn of Rachel, the favorite wife, has resulted in some stylish benefits for him (represented particularly by the sleeved robe), but has simultaneously produced intense anger and resentment among his siblings. This latter animosity is compounded by Joseph's bad "reports" on some of his brothers (is he a tale-bearer?) and his dreams of supremacy, so that resentment quickly festers into nothing less than raw hatred. His father even rebukes him for speaking of his dreams, perhaps being threatened himself by such affrontery to his own position. But the narrator also tells us that Jacob keeps the account of the dream of the sun, moon, and stars seriously in mind (37:11). This last point alerts the audience to the genuine potential of these dreams and intimates the exact nature of the reunion between father and son in Pharaoh's kingdom which climaxes the major movement of the story. It is indeed precisely around this separation and reunification that the story finally revolves. The drama opens, therefore, in the midst of both great love and profound hatred, and will ultimately close with all hatred being swallowed up in love, a love which remains consistently focused for the reader in the unfailing bond between father and son.

The story's next phase is transitional. Here the hero is carried from the lap of security into the heart of danger, there to be tested for his valor, cunning and faithfulness to the God of his fathers. Sent on a mission by his father to carry word back from the brothers in the distant fields, Joseph is quickly captured and threatened with death by his kinsmen. At this point the text becomes confused, with a conflation of accounts involving, on the one hand, the sale of Joseph to a caravan of Ishmaelites, and, on the other, a band of Midianite traders which discovers the lad in a pit and carries him off into Egypt. In either case, the primary focus seems to be on the close relationship between father and son. Reuben wants to "restore him to his father" (37:22), while Jacob's later encounter with the bloodied robe and his fearful mourning comprise the bulk of the end of the chapter. It is the narrator's concern for Jacob's deep personal commitment to Joseph which already provides the action with it's emotional center. We, the audience, anticipate that Jacob really need not mourn, but the pathos here is only greater for this fact. Because of this anticipation of Joseph's survival, we sense and share all the more in Jacob's later joy in seeing his son (Gen 46:29-30).

Next follows a series of dangerous tests for the untried hero. The important key to the final resolution of all this action is provided by the narrator's remark early in this section that Yahweh is "with Joseph" (39:2). In effect, at this juncture Yahweh as heavenly father takes the place of Jacob, the earthly father, who can only unknowingly suffer his son's apparent destruction. On this issue of Yahweh's care for Joseph, the narrator's sophistication is evident throughout the story, for this God never intrudes into the dramatic scheme as an actual actor within the plot's unfolding - as, for instance, he does in other tales where He stands among the dramatis personae. The Lord blesses the house of Joseph's Egyptian master (39:5), of course, but no interventions more direct than this are encountered in the story where Joseph himself is immediately involved.

The next chapters carry Joseph from early success to suffering and finally to consummate elevation as Pharaoh's chief minister or vizier. During his first successful position as Potiphar's overseer, the man's wife attempts to entice Joseph into her bed. We are told that Joseph was "handsome and good-looking", probably suggesting not only his champion qualities, but also his initiation into sexual awareness and the accompanying temptation which may deflect his highest heroic purposes. (The wife might be thought of as related mythically to Homer's Circe.) Her overtures fail, however, and she has the young man summarily tossed into prison as retribution.

Yet in this second, and perhaps lowest descent in the hero's fortunes, the narrator assures us that his tale will conclude favorably, for "the Lord was with Joseph and showed steadfast love, and gave his favor in the sight of the keeper of the prison" (39:21). It is precisely in prison, in fact, that Joseph is provided with the power which eventually vaults him quite meteorically out of the worst depths to the very pinnacle of glory within a single short step. We have here in these events, then, a signal instance of the mythic archetype of descent and ascent, humiliation and glorification. While incarcerated, he proves as able a leader as he had been a bondsman to Potiphar and is quickly placed in charge by the keeper. In this capacity, he meets the two figures who are to have much to do with this coming elevation, the Pharaoh's butler and baker, and reveals to the audience that he is now also as much a master of he interpretation of dreams as a dreamer himself. With God's guidance, he correctly predicts the butler's restoration, asking to be remembered to Pharaoh upon the resumption of his office. The butler's memory proves to be short, however, and the narrator informs us that he "forgot him" (40:23). This

12

passage contrasts explicitly and dramatically with the earlier "inside view" of Jacob's heart, where we were told that upon hearing the youth's dreams he "kept the saying in mind" (37:11). Once again, we are made to feel Joseph's pangs of loneliness away from his father, even though we are assured that Yahweh is guiding his steps.

Eventually, this phase of the story culminates and a new movement opens, when the Pharaoh dreams his own mysterious dreams of the fat and lean cows, and the contrasting ears of corn. Unable to find a competent interpreter, Pharaoh at last learns of Joseph through his repentant butler and sends for him from prison. Joseph, of course, then arrives and proceeds in lordly fashion to fulfill his now accustomed role as a dream reader. The narrator keeps our eye fixed upon the divine source of the young man's capacities, and so Joseph's speeches begin and end with his acknowledgment of God's omnipotence and surpassing regard for humankind (41:16, 25, 32). Pharaoh responds favorably to the prediction and, more interestingly, to the God who has acted in Joseph's life. Hearing that "a man discreet and wise" must be placed in charge to avert disaster, Pharaoh almost predictably then selects the very man who has brought this rather mixed news, to occupy the new office. Thus does a Hebrew who enters a foreign land in thrall become Egypt's second-in-command, eventually taking an Egyptian name and wife. So completely is Joseph absorbed into the culture thereafter that his first-born son, Manasseh, is named for the fact that God has made it possible for him to forget all his father's house (41:51), that dearest part of his life.

Another significant passage which indicates the narrator's conceptual skills is found in his observation that "Joseph went out from the presence of Pharaoh, and went through all the land of Egypt" (41:45-46). It seems likely that his is a triumphant counterpart to Joseph's earlier departure from Jacob's presence to visit what proves to be the "foreign" land of his brothers. In addition, not only does the hero ride abroad in regal style to oversee the harvests, he also in the end enjoys the remarkable position of having "all the earth" come to him for its agricultural needs (41:57). The seeker has now at last become the sought, the obedient hero now the hero to be obeyed. He has acquired what is an almost universal power, a power which he possesses because he has submitted his own will to faith in Yahweh's beneficent rulership. Yet the story is far from complete at this juncture; politics, with its harsh and gleaming symbols, stands only as an impersonal

13

prelude to the narrator's vision of the grander fulfillment of family reunification - the restoration and glorification of the sanctity of filial and fraternal piety. The young Joseph's dreams have yet to be fulfilled. Hence, at the very moment of the hero's finest material and cultural triumph, the reader is carried abruptly back to Palestine where a father named Jacob has Egypt and its resources much on his mind (42:1-5). Maximum effect is achieved by this juxtaposition. The father who has mourned a loss and now suffers from food shortages is soon to rejoice in a rejoining with one and the same son-supplier; yet only we in the audience anticipate this, and the tension within us builds as we look forward to what neither Jacob nor Joseph yet foresee.

In the next chapters, the plot is given over both to a detailed account of the intrigue which Joseph creates for his confused brothers, who have now entered his court to buy food, and to the anxiety provoked throughout the family over a series of trying events which foreshadow the revelation of Joseph's true identity. Joseph's motivations for concocting these ruses are not entirely clear. One possibility is that he may be driven by a combination of muted desire for retribution and a concern to make sure that his direct reunion with Benjamin and Jacob will occur. But perhaps Joseph also senses that only in the aftermath of a mock punishment will his brothers be able genuinely to accept his forgivenesss and welcome; only by truly accepting their guilt (42:21) are they psychologically and morally prepared to receive complete forgiveness. It is certain, moreover, that lingering doubts which the brothers have about the great ruler's real disposition toward them cause great fear after their father's death, a death which potentially frees Joseph from paternal judgment against fratricide (50:15-21). As Joseph later assures his brothers on that occasion, so it is the case during this masquerade, that he owes his life and position to God's goodness and protection, just as the brothers now also owe their own protection to God as they are controlled and manipulated by Joseph's hand. In spite of Joseph's later denial, he is "in the place of God" (50:19) in this specific sense, for as ascending hero he represents the purposes of the divine on earth.

Joseph carries out his masquerade over several sequences, raising the level of consternation in this family with each new turn. First, the brothers are accused of spying and placed in prison for three days; then, upon their release, Simeon is held captive as a guarantee for their return to Egypt with

14

Benjamin. This is, of course, a comic reversal of the brothers' earlier capture of Joseph, a misbegotten act which was to assure only suffering and regret for them and their father. In the midst of what seems to be only a higher stage of hardship, however, the reader knows that the brothers are on their way to their first genuine felicity. The narrator continues to tell his audience that it is the arm of the divine which masterfully operates here, having the brothers respond to Joseph's trick with the money in their grain sacks with the words, "What is this that God has done to us?" (42:28). Irony is raised to a new pitch at the conclusion of this sequence when Jacob appears in the scene once more to lament his loss of Joseph and to stand resolutely against Benjamin's departure - "he only is left" (42:38). The climactic recognition and reversal for the hero's father is now quickly approaching.

Finally, Jacob must relent before the famine and his sons depart southward with Benjamin in train. As the ruse continues, Joseph again meets his prostrated brothers, inquiring first after Jacob and then pouring out God's blessing upon his only full brother (43:27,29). After overcoming his momentary loss of composure in weeping for joy over Benjamin, he eats with (though apart from) his brothers in a weighty act of table hospitality, one which manifestly symbolizes the outpouring of God's righteous concern for them. The brothers then set out for home once more. Subsequently, the plot begins building to its first full climax, when Joseph's cup of divination is found in Benjamin's sack and the boy is soon after threatened with imminent slavery. Here it seems difficult not to predicate a measure of cruelty in Joseph, particularly since his younger brother, who is utterly guiltless, would have to be terrified throughout these proceedings. In any event, Judah indirectly confesses the brothers' guilt in the disappearance of the young Joseph (44:16) and goes on to conclude his plea for Benjamin with a pitiable evocation of Jacob's suffering. Here, we have the imaginative scene painted by Judah which finally closes the breach between Joseph and his brothers, a scene of a killing sorrow about to befall Joseph's father. The father's life, insists Judah, "is bound up in the lad's life" (44:30), and after having been wounded severely in Joseph's death, the loss of Benjamin will surely finish him. Thus, we see additional evidence of the centrality of Joseph's filial piety in the tale, part of a mutual love between father and son which outlasts and overthrows all intervening difficulties.

When Joseph, therefore, reveals his actual identity to his

15

kin in the overwhelming, capital announcement that he is a brother, it is the next question which focuses on the hero's central concern: "I am Joseph; is my father still alive?" (45:3). For Joseph, self-recognition is tantamount to the positive recognition of one's own sonship; the life of the father is life to the son. Nothing is so important after the fact of one's own life as the living breath of the parent who created that life. As Joseph goes on to explain to the brothers, it is God alone whose plan is being fulfilled in this sequence of events. He alone, says Joseph, "has made me a father to Pharaoh, and Lord of all his house and ruler over all the land of Egypt" (45:8). But even as Joseph's own "fatherhood" now places him in a position of consummate authority over his brothers and an entire nation, and even as the God of his fathers occupies an incomparably greater position over him and all creation, so now the major task for Joseph's brothers is to carry back word to their own father of his "splendor in Egypt". Hence, Joseph's important speech of self-revelation to his brothers reaches its real crescendo in the stress which is placed on transmitting the glorious news about Joseph to his father in their homeland. Joseph concludes his declaration in the following way: "And now your eyes see, and the eyes of my brother Benjamin see, that it is my mouth that speaks to you. You must tell my father of all my splendor in Egypt, and of all that you have seen. Make haste and bring my father down here" (45:12-13). As significant as the brothers' knowledge of him may be, that knowledge seems to have largely the function of bringing Jacob into Joseph's presence so that the father may at last truly see and hear his lost son.

It is only after this first obligation to the father is declared that the narrator finds it suitable to inform us that Joseph and Benjamin fall upon one another and weep for joy, along with the other brothers (45:14-15). Having made plans with Pharaoh's consent to return the entire family to Egypt in the land of Goshen (45:10; cf. 47:4-6), Joseph then sends his brothers on to Jacob. Thus does the father finally receive the word of life that Joseph thrives and rules. Following initial shock and disbelief, Jacob's spirit is wonderfully lifted by this extraordinary news as nothing else could possibly have done. And so he rejoices, "It is enough; Joseph my son is still alive; I will go and see him before I die" (45:28). The great love and respect which Joseph has consistently accorded his father is, therefore, now given back to him in a perfect reciprocity of affection.

This is the principal psychological and dramatic climax in

the story. Much action follows this, of course, including the eventual tearful reunion between father and son in Goshen (46:28-30). Yet in spite of the fact that the occasion of this meeting would seem to call for great words, the narrator essentially only repeats the speech which Jacob originally makes upon hearing that Joseph lives and prospers in Egypt. "Now let me die, since I have seen your face and know that you are still alive" (46:30). Prior to this event, we are presented in 46:1-4 with the divine confirmation of all that Joseph has said. On the way into Egypt, Jacob has an evening vision in which the early covenant promise to Abram is reiterated and assurance given that after his own entrance into Egypt, God will lead a great nation out of the land. (This is the sole instance of anything like a "direct" intrusion by God into the story-line.) The intimacy between father and son is also emphasized when God's speech concludes with the assurance that Joseph's own hand will one day close Jacob's eyes in death (46:4). Thus no later scene following Jacob's hearing first the blessed news quite issues in the same sense of internal resolution and peaceful consequence which one senses so powerfully here. The remainder of the drama seems to be a kind of concrete fulfilment, a progressive fleshing out, of the implications which flow directly from the life-saving message issuing from Egypt.

After a description of Joseph's masterly tactics in bringing all of Egypt's land and peoples eventually under Pharaoh's total monarchical control (Gen 47:20-26), the narrator once more redirects our attention to the father-son relation. Here we have the occasion of ceremonial parting between the two as death draws near for the elder. In this short section, Joseph swears a vow of loyalty to Jacob to carry him out of the present foreign territory and into their own homeland for burial (47:29-31). Jacob would join his own fathers in a deeply symbolic act of union and fealty even as Joseph and his father are finally once more united in life. It is no accident, however, that the long section dealing with Joseph's supreme service to the Pharaoh appears immediately before (or alongside of) this passage which brings Joseph and Jacob together in the old man's last days. The narrator is clearly demonstrating his literary skills, for we are meant to understand these two sets of relationships in terms of one another. Just as Joseph, the "lord of the land" (42:30), has proved eminently responsible in governing the Pharaoh's expansive kingdom - indeed, in saving "all" culture from starvation - so he assumes complete responsibility for his

17

father's final requirements. The loyalty which Jacob now ceremonially requests of him (47:29-31) is exactly the same loyalty already shown in abundance to the father-figure above him in Egypt, Pharaoh. At the same time, and precisely by virtue of these services, Joseph is understood to have achieved his own fatherhood or lordship, both as "a father to Pharaoh" (45:8) and as a righteous successor to Jacob as patriarch.

This fidelity to, and reverence for, Jacob is further manifested in the next section. Here Joseph has brought Ephraim and Manasseh, his two half-Egyptian sons, to his father for the deathbed blessing upon them. Within this scene emerges the last major climatic moment in the narrative. In this brief but emotion-drenched, portrait, Jacob kisses the grandsons and addresses Joseph in these words: "'I had not thought to see your face; and lo, God has let me see your children also'. Then Joseph removed them from his knees, and he bowed himself with his face to the earth" (48:11-12). It is rather easy to pass by this last phrase too hurriedly and to forget that it is none other than Joseph, the great lord of all Egypt, who is prostrating himself here: the same exalted leader - doubtlessly resplendent in his regal costuming, his heavy jewelry, and his magisterial retinue - who has brought all the surrounding civilized world to heel for the sake of the Pharaoh his "father". But such recognition only makes Joseph's solemn humility and loving respect all the more deeply moving, and declares the fundamental importance of this dimension of the story. In this act which so lionizes the tradition of filial piety among the ancients, we have the closing of the circle of images begun in Joseph's dreams of the subservience of the sun, moon, and stars before him. The hero's splendid elevation is achieved by virtue of his obedient service in the world governed by the God of his fathers, and is ritually completed in the respectful compliance and self-effacement symbolized in bowing low before the father for whom Elohim (God) is Lord.

The final chapter in the narrative begins with Joseph's responses to his father's death. Most of the material here is devoted to the faithful son's acts in carrying out Jacob's wish for burial in the land of Canaan. Actually, this chapter is divided into three fairly discrete sections. The initial long section reviews the burial in Canaan; the second repeats the brothers' concern that Joseph will one day take vengeance upon them for their evil deeds against him, particularly now that the father's potentially protective buffer has disappeared; the third reviews briefly Joseph's own long life, and focuses on his confidence that his expanding family will be led back into their native land. He requests that his own body be carried out when that time comes. In each case, it is the father-son relationship which establishes the dynamics for the narrator's creation of action and reflection.

After the explicit treatment of burial, the second section retains this special focus (50:15-20). Neither Jacob nor his other sons apparently feel unqualified confidence that Joseph's wrath will not break out against his half-brothers at a later time. So Jacob's request for clemency is reiterated in the aftermath of his death. In addition, the fidelity of the family to the God of the fathers is recited, with the brothers stressing their servitude to all three figures of power in their lives, Joseph, Jacob, and Elohim. Joseph, in turn, replies much as he had done when his identity was first revealed (45:4-8) - he will not presume to occupy the place of God in this matter. As the narrator has shown throughout, the essence of Joseph's heroic conduct is that he consistently and graciously defers to both father and God in questions of authority, precedence, and definitive interpretations. All that has transpired, insists Joseph, has been designed and carried out by God to save multitudes of people from harm. Joseph's heroism has, from first to last, been that which is granted to him by God, not that which, like some Prometheus, Antigone, or (to some extent) Odysseus, he has sought to acquire by virtue of his own strength or nobility.

In the final section, the same themes repeat, but in this culminating instance, Joseph has at last come to occupy the central position in the family. With Joseph's own death approaching, the narrator gives his indirect assurances that the respect which the son had regularly assigned to his father is now appropriately passed on to him. The story began with conflict between brothers, therefore, now concludes in a condition of harmony. At the last, Joseph himself becomes the great hero father - beyond even being "father" to Pharaoh - and is to be borne up out of Egypt to his father's land and blessed with honor by his sons and family. Because Joseph has proved so decisively to be the faithful son, the son of his father and of his God, he ultimately achieves the high status of a father in his own tradition and over all the sur- rounding land.

II

With this thematic outline of the story in mind, I now want

to mention specifically some of the more formal aspects of this piece of writing, aspects which relate the story to other literature both within and outside the Old Testament.

First, it is important to recognize that, in spite of various unique properties possessed by the narrative, it is of a piece with other expressions of Hebraic consciousness and concern. Throughout the composition, the narrator expresses through Joseph his own sturdy conclusion that God's providence and "hesed" (steadfast love) shape the world of creation and his elect people. For Joseph, man's meaning is finally and irrevocably discovered when God's meaning and intention for man is made manifest. Joseph's brothers never quite comprehend, as does he, that the entire scheme of history has been programmed to serve the high purposes of divinity; both Joseph's descent and ascent in the plot take their appropriate place when seen in this particular light. Yet the story is rather distinctive in the ancient Hebraic material because, with one exception, the presence of the divine is only asserted by Joseph or Jacob. God never makes a guest appearance in the action on his own, as is the case in much of the remainder of Genesis or in the Deuteronomic history (Joshua - Kings). In this respect, the Joseph story demonstrates some of the literary sophistication found later in the Book of Ruth, perhaps the most modern story in the Old Testament since its action occurs almost exclusively on the human plane.

As already indicated, the tradition of filial piety is another major fixture in this narrative. The respect owed to one's parents is an obligation and a virtue which receives consistent approbation in the Hebraic tradition. It is also a virtue widely accepted throughout the ancient world, from Greece to China. I have wanted to show here how a story which is often read solely for its description of Joseph's adventures with his brothers and in Egypt can actually be more properly interpreted from within this tradition. The heroism of Joseph is not understood to be a matter of autonomous separation and elevation beyond the life of the family. Heroism is rather constituted precisely by the extent to which one's own father is consistently honored in life and the will of God both sought and obeyed. In this regard, it is also very important to note that we learn almost nothing of Joseph's personal relations with any of the Egyptians, including Pharaoh and his own wife. Only the brief tale of his encounter with Potiphar's wife provides us inside information of the sort we regularly receive when the narrator is portraying Joseph in the company of, or commenting on, his father and brothers.

Third, this story is undergirded by the same confidence in God's support for the righteous that we associate with the Deuteronomic historian (Joshua - Kings) and the prophetic writings. The thoughts and actions of a single righteous man affect events for good far beyond the capabilities of his own immediate powers. This concept is bound up with, and helps to support, the covenantal theory of social organization and responsibility which increasingly characterized the life of Israel after the enunciation of the Law at Sinai. In this earlier instance of God's response to the quest for moral uprightness in Joseph's experience, the narrator has been attentive to the salvific effects on the hero himself, as well as on the familial society which benefits from Joseph's goodness.

Finally, we have the significant theme of the "stranger in a strange land" being played out in this narrative. From Abram's journey into a foreign land assigned to him by God, to the Egyptian bondage, and on to the Assyrian and Babylonian captivities, the Old Testament reflects the Hebrew people's experience of finding themselves to be foreigners in difficult and unfriendly circumstances. Perhaps in part because of such experience, an important tradition amongst ancient Israelites sought to protect the interests of the stranger or the foreigner in their midst. Having been many times the trod-upon contingent of society themselves, they were particularly sensitive to the plight of the stranger in their own camp. Deut 10:18-19 may serve as a summary of this tradition; describing the covenant relationship, the text states that Yahweh "executes justice for the fatherless and the widow, and loves the sojourner, giving him food and clothing. Love the sojourner therefore; for you were sojourners in the land of Egypt". In the Joseph story, however, the emphasis is not upon the sufferings of an immigrant group, but upon the marvellous hospitality which God opens to Jacob's family through the elevation of the hero from stranger to powerful celebrity. Joseph becomes an archetype for the divine beneficence graciously extended to all who would serve justly, even in an alien landscape, within the care of God.

Next, I shall comment on some of the significant literary and mythic patterns which emerge from the story.

First, the work is clearly a comedy, which is to say that the scheme of action carries the hero to an ultimate reconciliation with self, family, and environment. Whatever tribulations he is summoned to endure during the story, the comic hero is one who emerges at last from all challenging events, chastened but victorious. By contrast, the tragic mode typically follows a course of action which delivers the hero from security and reputation to disaster and shame; genuine tragic heroes are actually quite rare in the Old Testament, however, for it is, by and large, the "heroes of faith" who dominate these writings. Perhaps Saul, Samson, and Jeremiah might be regarded as figures within one or another sort of modified tragical framework. But if so, one would have to choose criteria other than just those offered by Aristotle's concept of the tragic hero in order to delineate this case. Within the Joseph story, though, there remains no room whatever for tragic interpretation.

The serious comedy will often begin with the hero in a condition of relative security, continue with a period of significant trial and testing, and conclude with the central character being restored or elevated again to a condition of felicity, a condition morally superior to his point of origin. The concluding stage in this, of course, also bears a resemblance to the archetypal outline of the so-called "quest" myth. According to Northrop Frye and others, this is the dominant myth in all of literature. Its aim is to bring the conscious and unconscious aspects of the self into harmony, to develop an ideal relation between the apotheosis of the hero and an omnipotent personal community, and to integrate every level of the created world - human to mineral - into an ideal or golden order. States Frye, "It corresponds to, and is usually found in the form of, the vision of the unfallen world or heaven in religion. We may call it the comic vision of life, in contrast to the tragic vision, which sees the quest only in the form of its ordained circle".[2] The Joseph story clearly aims to lead its audience toward, and assure it of, such a vision of completed harmonization between all aspects of the personal and social order. Joseph has endured a variety of difficulties in order to bring his family into a secure and bounteous relationship with itself, and to seal the old, but unwavering, links between the father and son in a culminating display of perfect piety. In addition, he has created an ideal condition of state for the Egyptian aristocracy, with all the inhabitants both provided with food and brought under the complete dominance of Pharaoh as his slaves. Although the story ends with the hero's death, the mood of that ending only reinforces the controlled dignity, calm and confidence which is featured in the last scenes. In spite of lying now embalmed in his coffin, the hero retains an aura or presence which, one senses, continues to live on for some time within the kingdom of divinely ordained harmony which his mediatory agency has brought into being for all.

The great mythic ritual called "rite of passage" might also be mentioned here. The story's three-part movement, from childhood innocence, via dangerous trial and the demand for new skills, into full adulthood, is an excellent example of this myth of initiation. Joseph Campbell has even termed this pattern a "monomyth", so abundant are its instances within the literature of both ancient and modern man.[3] Joseph resembles numerous other mythic and literary figures who are obliged or compelled to pass through a series of proofs and tests of emerging manhood before being finally accepted by the gods or received back into their societal life. Such examples as Theseus, Icarus, Natty Bumppo, and William Faulkner's Ike McCaslin come quickly to mind here. During his capture by his brothers and his thralldom in the hands of the Midianites, during his sexual temptation and then his imprisonment under Pharaoh's guard, the hero passes through the crucial period of isolation and intimidation provided by the myth. Once Joseph has successfully negotiated this obstacle, the world beyond calls him back unto itself and the social order accepts him and stands in happy submission to his authority. This central phase of the myth has been given special attention within the realm of cultural anthropology by Victor Turner, who has explicitly distinguished three steps in the complete process of initiation: separation, liminality, and reaggregation.[4] The hero's separation from, and reunion with, Jacob can be understood appropriately within this framework as well, for the father-son relationship (especially the son's religious training) establishes the background for Joseph to survive the separation; it is also the ideal goal toward which the rite of initiation moves, demonstrating the worthiness of the son to share finally in the father's prestige and to take up his mantle of authority. Joseph, therefore, is the hero who progresses from probably presumptuous innocence through a period of grave hardship in order to prove his courage and valor genuine, and his imagination resourceful. In this story, however, he is far more than this - indeed, this description alone would be a complete theological falsification of the message which the narrator wants the tale to bear for his audience. Joseph's heroism is not a function of his individual powers of body and mind, but is entirely the result of his obedience and service to the God of his father. All autonomy is strictly subordinated to social theology and to sacred piety under the hegemony of the divine government.

As a final clarifying comment here, we might graph the pattern of action in the story in the following way:

Home

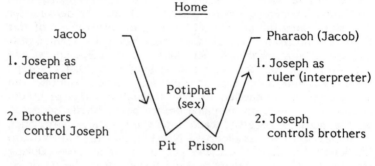

Jacob — Pharaoh (Jacob)

1. Joseph as dreamer   1. Joseph as ruler (interpreter)

Potiphar (sex)

2. Brothers control Joseph   2. Joseph controls brothers

Pit   Prison

Away from Home

In this diagram we notice immediately the movement which is initiated from an original high point, then proceeds down into the darkness of difficulty (or "deep sea journey" - Campbell), through a time of severe trial, and finally back up and out to a second, superior pinnacle. We have here then, at least in part, an Old Testament version of the "Divina Comedia" or of "Pilgrim's Progress". Almost instantly, we recognize the perfect structural symmetry of the story, with one nadir complementing or balancing each summit, and a short, but tentative and ambiguous, rise in fortune standing in the very center. The story begins and ends with Joseph's identity and status being determined by his relation to the highest authority figures on the historical plane, Jacob and Pharaoh (though we see that for the narrator, Jacob actually appears to hold the higher of the two positions when they are placed together; see 47:7-10). The most distinctive of Joseph's talents, his clairvoyance, also owns a notable place within this symmetry. On the one hand, the hero presents himself as a youthful, provocative dreamer, while on the other, he is found to be an increasingly mature interpreter of dreams, a diviner, and perhaps even a kind of shaman. The former capacity leads him directly into the torment of captivity and isolation, the latter, out of prison and into glory and distinction. On each side of the pattern, one can also observe that the relation between Joseph and his brothers inverts.

From a youth hated by, and finally maliciously controlled by, his brothers, Joseph becomes, on the opposite side of the chasm and at the successful completion of his initiation, the man who is loved and feared by them, one who now quite completely controls them.

In the center we find the low points in Joseph's odyssey - the pit and the prison - which correspond negatively to the ideal conditions located on each side of the overall pattern, the one a horror created by his own family, the other generated by false testimony and sexual intrigue in a foreign land. In both of these unfortunate situations, he is a stranger "away from home", in a liminal condition where all securities have summarily vanished. By contrast, at the beginning and end of the story, the hero is entirely "at home". Between these pairs exists the momentary inflation which threatens the hero with complete destruction, or at least a loss of sight of his truest goals - personal purity and service to God; the temptation here, fittingly enough, is the sexual one, the one normal to crisis in the adolescent stage of development and the one in this story which portends a short-circuiting of the movement toward a perfected conclusion.

Most importantly, however, the twin peaks in Joseph's career represent his loving relationship with his father. From Jacob's own house his adventures unfold; out of his father's warm attentions come the son's capacities to maintain his righteous life and his eventual desire to re-establish the old family. Toward a reunion with his father the remainder of the story also carefully wends its way. And in their reconciliation flowers a full vision of the virtue of filial piety which is the condition of Joseph's successful rulership in Egypt and his faithful assumption of the head of his original household.

Chapter Two

WOUNDED BEGINNINGS: DAVID AND TWO SONS

Burke O. Long

Ecularization in our culture may be signaled by our easy acquiescence to divided human experience, a house with many single rooms, or an atom split into its tiny components. A sign of spirituality may be the converse: the lively sense of patterned inter-relationship in human events - like the web of energies physicists now imagine at the heart of material reality.

Wherever they may be found, sacred scriptures seem to supply those patterns by which fragile creatures measure their wondrous experience. In our culture, historically speaking, many of the paradigms were in the Bible, that strange collection of books within books that has moved people, often unawares, to find streams of intentionality running deep in human aspiration, defeat, good, and even folly. Sometimes the stories spoke of divine intervention in the life of one who was unsuspecting: a rogue (Jacob, Samson), a good and pious man (Noah, Moses, Paul), an unlikely shepherd (Amos), a mother (Hannah, Mary). And one must have wondered if he could be that rogue, or she that woman blessed among women. At other times, these Biblical stories suggested covert patterning - strange avatars of distant mythic paradigms: the passing over the river Jordan imagined as a second exodus by a new Moses, splendidly untethered by time and space; the collapse of Jericho's walls in seven days, as though turning a myth of creation in on itself, a sabbatical reversion to chaos; or the man-son hanging sacrificed on a rough hewn tree, resonating to the mysterious song of the first-born slain for dark reasons (Genesis 22; Exodus 12-13). And one must have wanted to be that son on whom the promise, or the world, depended.

If at all, modern ears probably hear best some such covert patterning if not just these. We are accustomed to hearing of storied worlds peopled with secular heroes or anti-heroes, where gods give no direction, and where the myths of Freud and Jung find incarnation and repetition in driven characters. And yet both ways of patterning - the public divine intervention, and the covert playing out of typologies, are deeply Biblical. Perhaps it is only in our modern world, that is, in the kind of narrative universe created apart from divine intervention, that one can sense the deep psychic roots of covert patterning, and of the human yearning for sense. As though we human creatures will have our order from chaos and our remediality for good. Crumbs are less sustaining than the well-turned loaf.

The story of Amnon, Tamar, David and Absalom in 2 Samuel 13-14 is but a chapter from a larger whole, a Hebrew "Roman fleuve", that noble chronicling of King David. Yet it is an episode which in itself is satisfying and complete - offering us intense drama in calculated fratricide and measured relief in a father-son kiss. The story is family centered. It has to do with private rape, revenge and reconciliation. Yet, it is a story of the royal family, whose affairs seem to have had vital public relevance in ancient Israel. So the story of rape and revenge is also the beginning of anxiety about the kingdom, and of how Absalom reaches for the crown. But where events touch our deeper passions, the tale tells of twisted human relationships and wounded beginnings, as though from brokenness comes wholeness, a larger pattern more satisfying to the soul.[1]

In the beginning, brushed up like wisps on canvas, we see a three-way bond: brother and sister, Absalom and Tamar, children of David, and Amnon, a son of David (see 2 Sam 3:2-3). Amnon loved his half sister, Tamar. Amnon is in fact lovesick. He is drawn to this very beautiful virgin, but she is quite inaccessible. That is the torment. Amnon must suppose that the laws regulating marriage among kin (Lev 18:9) and protecting marriageable women (Deut 22:23-29) stand in his way. Ironically, Tamar herself, under attack and desperate, will suggest that royal families have ways to circumvent custom (2 Sam 13:13). Amnon is frustrated and vulnerable to the suggestions of his friend Jonadab, who is a "very crafty man".

Amnon listens: "lie down on your bed and pretend to be ill; and when your father comes to see you, say to him 'Let my sister Tamar come and give me bread to eat, and prepare food in my sight, that I may see it, and eat from her hands'".

Understanding perfectly what drives Amnon, Jonadab speaks of calculated deception. He need say nothing about singleminded pursuit. Amnon readily agrees to the plan and speaks to the king, who then orders his daughter to go to Amnon's house to prepare food. The swiftly told action suddenly slows with great dramatic effect. Speech gives way to watching: "...she took dough, and kneaded it, and made cakes in his sight, and baked the cakes. And she took the pan and emptied it out before him, but he refused to eat" (vv 8-9). We are made to linger, to watch Tamar, joining Amnon in his voyeuristic pleasure.

This pause has in fact been subtly prepared by a pattern of repetition and omission. Early on, Jonadab mentioned the word "look" and hinted at the "watching" that was to come: "Let my sister Tamar come and give me bread to eat and prepare food before my eyes, that I may look at it (her)[2] and eat from her hand" (13:5). When repeated to King David, that ambiguity is gone: "Pray let my sister come and make a couple of cakes before my eyes, that I may eat from her hand" (13:6). David then commands Tamar, but, apparently suspecting nothing, drops every allusion to "looking", saying simply, "Go to you brother Amnon's house, and prepare food for him" (13:7). Having gradually disappeared from the story, the allusions to "looking" reassert themselves with sudden and dramatic force when Tamar comes before her half-brother (13:8-9). But we are not hearing the words of "looking", we are looking, watching along with Amnon.[3]

The lovesick brother turned pursuer now turns voyeur, as though savoring the mere sight of his beautiful half-sister. It is also that menacing, deadly playful pause before attack. Tamar is not a sister, after all. She is more an obstacle nearly overcome, or a victim within reach. As the brother in our eyes becomes rapist, so the sister in her brother's eyes becomes victim. And bonds of family and taboos of society, like weakly held conviction, become as nothing.

Amnon in fact ignores Tamar's plaintive resistance (v 14), and "being stronger than she, he forced her, and lay with her". Then after the violence is done, he thrusts aside her legitimate claims to marriage (Deut 22:29). For the rapist now hates his victim more than he loved her, in ways at once more violent and cruel. He casts her out with contempt, a used and nameless woman. The Hebrew is graphic: "Put this (female thing) away from me" (v 17). Tamar is twice the victim: once as the prize of brother become rapist, a second time as though a symbol of rapist turned self-hater. As before, speech gives way to strong visual images: "So his servant put her out and bolted the door after her. And Tamar put ashes on her head, and rent the long robe which she wore; and she laid her hand on her head, and went away, crying aloud as she went". Events completely reverse Tamar's fortunes. We watch not a beautiful young woman, but a woman become old in her desolation, wearing the shredded tokens of a bereaved widow without ever having been a wife.

Expected familial relations have come unraveled and been twisted again into grotesque, private obscenity. And with such calculated effect! We are caught off guard in a sense. Lazed into the family bonds by excessive numbers of sibling, brother-sister terms, how shocking to taste the terrifying irony of those same words in a deed of brotherly violence.[4] Amnon already savors Tamar as lover and victim (vv 8-9), but the innocent Tamar still looks upon Amnon as a brother in need of care. Courtly language is merely formal, as though better to hide the horror. Even after Amnon's plan is clear to her, for Tamar protests and resists, she still calls upon her "brother", all the while knowing with whom she is really having to deal. Finally, the arrow of violent intent flies with sure aim, thrust at the reality of brother-sister. The injury is deep, and the sibling words, now sham, disappear (vv 14-15, 17-19). It is degredation without remedy, a break without reconciliation, told starkly, truly, quite without moralizing.

Like a passing tone which robs of final resolution, we are carried through Tamar's desolation within range of another triangular bond: brothers Absalom and Amnon, father David. As in the first episode, the situation is understated and highly suggestive: Absalom curiously belying the depths of Tamar's tragedy while carrying a secret hate for his brother; father David, invoked in weakness - simply "very angry".[5] For the moment we only dimly suspect the inner charge which will power the drama. A secret hate, carried in silence (he spoke "neither good nor bad"; cf. Gen 31:24, 29), suggesting a harbored intent to avenge the ignominy put on his sister. Where Amnon had been the pursuer, he is now to become the pursued, but unwittingly.

Biding his time for two years, Absalom finds a moment to engineer his revenge. The occasion: a sheepshearing festival. The guests: all the king's sons, the better to conceal Absalom's singular interest. It takes a bit of doing to get Amnon to attend - a devious invitation to the king himself, and when refused, a more pressing demand that Amnon, who by circumstances has become the crown prince, attend as a royal representative. King David is guarded and circumspect, as though suspicious, or as though drawing back from manipulative overtures which mirror his own action towards the innocent Uriah (2 Samuel 11). Finally, David relents and allows Amnon to go. Absalom then moves quickly to order his brother's murder. It is brother against brother, avenger of sister's honor.

But is it the noblest of deeds after all? Absalom charges his servants: "When I say to you, 'strike Amnon', then kill him. Fear not. Is it not that I command you (hălō᾽ kî ᾽ānōkî)? Be courageous and be valiant (hizkû wihĕyû libnê-ḥayîl; 13:28)". There is just the hint of royal prerogative in these words. With a similar speech David had solicited the political and personal loyalty of the men from Jabesh Gilead: "Let your hands be strong, and be valiant (teḥĕzaqnāh yĕdêkem wihĕyû libnê-ḥayîl; 2 Sam 2:7)". And Israel's very first king had sought David's personal loyalty amid his own growing distrust and fear of a challenge: "Be valiant for me (hĕyēh lî lĕben-ḥāyîl; 1 Sam 18:17)". With similar words, Solomon will test the loyalty of a rival contender to the throne: "If he prove to be a valiant man (yihyeh lĕben-ḥāyîl), not one of his hairs shall fall to the earth" (1 Kgs 1:52). So Absalom's heart perhaps is as swelled with ambition as it is darkened with hate. The moment suggests that Absalom had long ago savored this fortuitous opportunity to become crown prince under the pretext of brother's revenge.[6] Apparently, then, with double intent, the deed is done. Brother strikes brother - the one wronged in family honor by his sister's dishonor, the other murdered to satisfy that honor and to further a secret ambition. The one opportunistic, the other a victim, having once been the victor. Absalom is Cain redivivus who just as decisively, if less impetuously, ruptures the fabric of family.

Almost immediately word comes to King David, and he reacts as though his worst suspicions had been realized in fact. Superimposed images repeatedly flash before our eyes, fixing us on this moment. The murderer flees, while intensely shared mourning engulfs the court - first mistakenly for all the sons, then focuses on the one son, Amnon, the heir apparent. It is as though while Absalom flees, the wailing grows louder and louder: "...the king's sons came and lifted up their voice and wept; and the king also, and all his servants wept very bitterly" (13:36; see 37b). A grief shared by so many so deeply (while Absalom flees) - and all the more wrenching for the utter contrast with Tamar's sorrow which was borne by none save herself (while Absalom flees).[7]

Gradually our attention turns from father and sons, to father and two particular sons: the one dead, the other in flight. At this point, it is a question of being comforted in the death of the one and reconciled in life to the other. The king mourns. Yet hesitatingly, apparently in private, and lacking energy sufficient for decisive action, David longs for the living, seeing Amnon is dead. Absalom, Cain-brother-murderer, has become in fact the eldest son, the crown prince, in exile - even if it is self-imposed. The king is without his son and the kingdom without its proper heir.

Joab sees this fact clearly but moves indirectly, preferring to have a "wise woman" put the point to the but dimly aware David. Here our watching gives way to listening, as this woman persistently brings her case before the king. It is a sparring match of sorts. She indirectly, gently, politely, presses the king to decide the fate of her son. As though reluctant to deal with the central issue, the king finally gives in to this courtly cajolery, and swears to save the son. As once before (12:1-6), David has unwittingly judged his own actions. Still gently and with consummate Oriental politeness, the "wise woman" reveals to the king that her story was really a kind of parable of the king's own situation. Her speech opens and closes curtains, teasing truth out of fiction. She plainly states the point: "the king convicts himself, inasmuch as the king does not bring his banished one home again". Then she abruptly obscures the matter again saying: "...for the king will hear, and deliver his servant from the hand of the man who would destroy me and my son" (v 16). This climactic statement is high irony. It refers to the "case" which the king now knows is fictitious. And at the same time, it accuses the king himself, who is asked to spare this woman and the "people of God" from himself, that is, from the consequences of his own inaction. Fiction has revealed truth (the banished one endangers the public life of the kingdom) and truth in its turn has laid bare the fiction (the woman's petition before the king). Nothing more need be said, to the king, or to us who have learned the truth along with him. It is now only a question of who is responsible for this ruse, and of acting on its truth.

Just here, being taught by this wise woman, we become aware of the double focus for the entire story. It is clear now in the exile of this son, this next son in line for the throne, that the drama is really summed up in the struggle of David to reconcile the interests of family and state. David is a father, sketched in shadows as a man who is angry but holds back the hand stretched out against his son, a man who grieves deeply for the one son and closes his heart to the other, a man easily decisive in some circumstances, immobilized and blind in others. But also king. His family troubles rupture the dreams of his subjects, and threaten the harmony of the state. And he must be shown this, astonishingly enough.

The scene abruptly shifts. Joab is summoned, and having taken full responsibility for the situation, is commanded to bring the son, Cain-brother-murderer-crown prince, back to his father. Swiftly, the son returns, but to a cautious, strangely distant reconciliation: "Let him dwell apart in his own house; he is not to come into my presence" (14:24). But this does not suit the impetuous Absalom. He acts decisively after two years - as in the move against Amnon - impatiently seeking, and getting, audience with the king. We watch, then, a full reconciliation between father and son, one which comes after three years in exile in Geshur, and two years in his own house. Five years apart from his father, and yet a reconciliation of little emotional excess, told with great restraint: "So he came to the king, and bowed himself on his face to the ground before the king; and the king kissed Absalom" (14:33). How controlled a reconciliation it is! As though the unease between them could not be overcome, even with a kiss. After all, spilt blood cannot be so easily forgot. Nor can we, who have heard the narrator's panegyric to Absalom in 14:24-27, fail to hear the echo of rivalry between an earlier king and a handsome young man (Saul and David; 1 Sam 16:12, 18-19).

In reality, the reconciliation of son with father and the settling of the affairs of the kingdom are both overshadowed by the manipulative, impetuous Absalom and the wariness with which he is treated. Once bitten, twice shy, as the saying goes. Even Joab, having succeeded in bringing Absalom back, is curiously inattentive (14:29). So David's wordless gesture of affection at the end is exquisite because it says little and says much. Absalom has returned, father is united with son, the kingdom has its proper heir. But innocence, once lost, can never be regained. The story which began in the dark of Amnon's lusting heart, ends in the light-shadow of Absalom's move to center stage - the obedient son who nonetheless barely hides his ruthless willingness to take what he wants.

This tale is among the most powerful stories in the Old

Testament. Undoubtedly, much of its appeal is in the universality of its themes; yet themes alone cannot account for literary power.

The story is effective also because of the author's sure sense of style and pace. We pass through two worlds: the hectic violence of rape and revenge gives way suddenly to slow, measured awakening when the king meets a "wise woman". In her wily talk lies the power for reconciliation of father and son; for us, her clever cajolery gives relief and humor - well spoken, leisurely wizardry in contrast to men driven by elemental passions.

Elsewhere in the story, our pace slows and quickens at crucial moments, giving pause, emphasis, or nuance. When Tamar enters Amnon's house, action and talk slows considerably. Speech gives way to wordless watching, as though the very triviality of making bread is important to the story (13:8-9). And so it is. The scene quietly pictures the servile, menial ordinariness of this woman in contrast to the fantasy-heavy world of Amnon's lovesick desires. We pause and see Tamar as an irresistably enchanting scullery maid. Similarly, after the stunning quickness of brother-murder, the pace slows again, this time to intensify the grief of king-father for his son-heir (13:30-37). We may note also the pause to give adulatory comment on this restored heir, Absalom. The narrator speaks an aside to an audience, the better to say who this man now is: the royal prince, first in rank and beauty, made in the image of King David (14:24-27). All these instances of slackened pace, flanked as they are 'fore and aft" by quick, decisive, even violent action, force us to linger, to feel an emphasis, to catch a nuance, to be caught by events.

The story gains power, too, from its epic proportions. How subtly the tale of the king's children becomes a drama of the kingdom, or always was and is so! In striking his brother, Absalom is Cain redivivus; but we sense hidden ambition, and in fleeing the angry wrath of his father, Absalom-Cain, brother-murderer, becomes exiled crown prince. King David, angry father who grieves in public and privately refuses to forgive, in effect clouds the prospect of orderly succession. His indecision threatens the cosmos of kingdom with the chaos of an empty throne.

Chaos and cosmos; disruption and restoration. The images resonate deeply in the Biblical tradition. We must gaze further, and see more deeply.

This episode is a story within a story. The king's sons are

33

like their father in many ways, and already in the private actions of father and king one has seen - like some sort of dreaded premonition - the deeds of sons and heirs. One may say that the private actions of David and Bathsheba (2 Samuel 11-12) set in motion a series of events, brought forth like caricatured offspring. The child of adultery dies, but another is born. One son rapes one of David's daughters, and another revenges the act. This same son Absalom seizes his father's throne, but is finally ignominiously slain, his revolution aborted by the same man who earlier had effected reconciliation. Now two more sons can compete for the crown, the one (Adonijah; 1 Kings 1-2) grasping after their father's concubine, and being murdered by the other, a ghastly act which nonetheless gives birth to an era of stability (Solomon). Stories within stories, and within a story: as though what is sown at the beginning is reaped throughout, like a curse from which one is never free.[8]

But also we may see that a disturbance in private leads inexorably to public disruption, which then flows back into reconciliation, only to begin the cycle again. Thus, those events which on one level appear as an ordinary progression of human deeds seem also to express in their interior depths an archetypal pattern: harmony → disruption → restoration. Or, cosmos → chaos → cosmos. It is the Genesis story in another dress. Created harmony goes awry in the garden, spreading decay in the world, only to be washed away in forty days of rain: restoration and new beginning.[9] So too with David and his family. What begins in harmony is disrupted in private grasping for Bathsheba, but is restored in the birth of a son "beloved of the Lord" (2 Sam 12:25). And this is a cycle to be replicated in the sons - the disruptive chaos or private obscenity leads finally to wholeness (cosmos) in the reconciliation of father and son. It is an understated reconciliation, however, or a chastened cosmos. Having lived so deeply, both David and Absalom must begin again, wounded and vulnerable to the inexorable knotting that binds them together. The cycle repeats in Absalom's brash attempts to gain the crown. And so too his younger brother, Adonijah.

We touch perhaps the central aspect of this story's power here. The events not only intertwine, and replicate, and so work out the convoluted trail of human tragedy. They also enact a deeply Biblical, and one might say, human pattern: the struggle for cosmos in the midst of chaos, or the repeated, incessant, driven, attempts to make whole what continues to be experienced as disrupted. In Biblical terms, this struggle is fundamentally religious, for in its storied embodiment the name Israel means one who has "striven with God and men, and prevailed" (Gen 32:28).

Chapter Three

MOSES

James Nohrnberg

Hen it is represented in a text, heroism may be called the prime cultural symbol of the formation of the human individual. Typically, to become a "hero" is to transcend or eclipse one sort of being by another, to shape a "self" different from that of other men. So long as such definition does not imply that heroism does violence to distinctions between God and man, or that heroism is the deification of self-reliance, the Bible offers us many heroes. A selfish hero like Jacob, however, may be thought to be the less heroic, the more selfish he is. And a mighty hero like Samson may be thought to be more, not less, vulnerable for the possession of his exceptional gift. In this essay I shall explore the Biblical perception of another "hero" - Moses: a hero whose individuality is dissolved in his office, and whose life is almost totally conscripted by the history of Israel.

Giants in Time[1]

The Bible does not offer us demi-gods and supermen. It accordingly circumvents the so-called "heroic age", the age that imaginative historiography places between an age of the gods and an age of the people.[2] There seem, however, to be two traces of the "heroic age" in the Bible. One is the giants (Gen 6:1-4): but their story illustrates dangers analogous to the merging of heaven and earth in the Flood story; they defy, as it were, the laws of nature; theirs is a heroic age God cancelled.

The other trace also suggests heroic size, in this case size as conferred by length of life. God moves to limit this at the same time that he destroys the generation of the giants, but nonetheless the longevity of our progenitors is inherited by

Abraham and Moses. Very long-lived characters, of course, do not initially suggest heroism, but longevity can serve to make a hero a "giant in time", a corporate personality who contains within his own life-span generations of his people. We shall see that Moses' life spans a distinctive period in Israel's "history". It is a Mosaic period, for perceptions of its distinctiveness cannot be dissociated from perceptions of Moses himself. Moses' long life is thus commensurate with an "age". In a sense, therefore, the Mosaic "life story", occupying as it does the limits of a "period", is offered to us in place of, and in the form of, a "heroic age".

The Birth of the Life of Moses

The Book of Exodus begins before the birth of Moses, and the exodus it describes is not fully realized until after Moses dies. And yet the understanding of the exodus-event is surely "through Moses", and we may begin from a study of his life story: it is one way of approaching what we shall finally call the genesis of the exodus.

Moses is a hero, and the hero's life is determined by a principle of heroic singularity. The presence of this principle in the Bible is manifested by four heroic origins: a beginning from conception, from birth, from conversion, and from - as we say - nowhere. The resulting narratives are the annunciation-story, the birth-story, the call-story, and the allusion (for no "story" can develop here) to the obscurity or exceptional unlikelihood of the candidate for heroism, or to the hero's oddity (the least of his tribe; "Can anything good come out of Nazareth?" and so forth). Each of the "origins" may be colored by the others: for example, a prophet who is "called from the womb" enjoys a vestigial conception-story, as well as his call-story - his calling is, as it were, hereditary. Similarly, a conception or a birth in adverse or humble circumstances counts as an obscurity-allusion. A child born to a barren or virginal mother, to whom the conception is announced and who bears in obscure circumstances and who dedicates the child to a calling or receives an announcement of his calling - would enjoy the blessing of all four "origins". The more complete the cycle, the more something larger than the advent of the individual hero is betokened. Samuel, called repeatedly, is called from the womb by an annunciation story, and his call disestablishes the sons of Eli, whose house administers the temple where Samuel is called. Vision and word are at low ebb in Eli's time, and prophets are not yet called prophets: thus the call of Samuel is not only

Samuel's, but that of prophecy itself, and especially of the king-making and king-unmaking prophet who is twin-born with the monarchy.

The only annunciatory motif in Moses' birth story is the giving of his name, but it has been displaced from any annunciatory position, and it does not make him a savior, but a saved one. The birth-story is otherwise determined by its mediation of the polarity Hebrew/Egyptian, and in this it anticipates the almost constitutive role Pharaoh will have towards Moses. Moses' singularity is that he is a Hebrew Egyptian and an Egyptian Hebrew: in him are combined what the exodus will separate. His birth is designed to create this interface. Destined to be thrown in the Nile by the edict of Exod 1:22, Moses has his life saved by his mother's exposing him on the river. On the one hand, the bondwoman's son is destined to be adopted by the Pharaoh's maternally-inclined daughter, just as his fellow Hebrews are conscripted for Pharaoh's work. On the other hand, the bondwoman is able to hire herself out as the child's nurse, and is thus re-instated as the child's mother: the servants are doing the masters' living for them. The trace of an adoption-formula in the Princess' commission, "Take this child" (cf. Exod 6:7, "I will take you for my people"), shows that she only adopts the child to put it up for adoption, and so must further establish Moses as "foundling", even while his mother recovers for him the status of "son".

The birth-story sequence illustrates a much vaster pattern than its own, a story stretching from Joseph to Joshua, of which it is first recapitulatory and then prefigurative: (1) birth in "Israel"; (2) immersion in Egypt; (3) appeal to the ruling house in Egypt (Moses "appeals" to the daughter from the river; he appeals to Pharaoh by the river [Exod 7:15]); (4) negotiation with the ruling house; (5) restoration to "Israel". As the mother's taking of wages from Pharaoh's daughter shows, the ultimate "plundering of the Egyptians" is already implicit in this, the most nuclear version of the story pattern.

The story of Moses' birth belongs to a widely distributed story-type, even though it seems to challenge that type at every point. The type is the "rags to riches" story: a rejected but potentially royal - or a technically royal but disinherited or rejected or endangered - child, is cast out or exposed, thereby becoming a foundling. (He is typically found in package-form: swaddled, bundled, boxed, cribbed, encapsulated, or bound.) The child is rescued from exposure and succored, or guarded, or preserved, or adopted, by rustics, servants, animal-tenders, animals, or some socially marginal being - or by a god. He is reared "abroad", that is, during the period of rustication; he grows capable and "goodly", and then returns to his "home", either succeeding to honors, recognition, his original high status in the ascendant social class, or earning promotion or vindication and removing his stigma while regaining his identity. In Neo-Platonic allegorizations of it, this romance stands for the descent and return of the soul - and indeed descent themes are not far from the Biblical story in its enlarged form (Joseph to Joshua), which encompasses both the descent of Jacob-Israel to the "Sheol" or shadow-world of Egypt, and the finding and protecting of the foundling Israel in the wilderness.

Now as this paradigm applies to Moses, we can only note that it is turned inside out. Moses is not a royal/rejected child; he is a desired/low-born child. He is not abandoned by his parent, but preserved - or rather he is "abandoned" under careful supervision. He is exposed not so much to the elements, as to the literary motif of exposure! He is not the child of the Princess, even if he might be. He is reared first by his mother, and thereafter in unspecified circumstances that make him appear to be "Egyptian". He is then adopted a second time, as an adult, by his father-in-law; only then is he found sojourning among shepherds - when he has become a father himself, and can name his own son, again according to the motif ("he called his name Gershom; for he said, 'I have been a sojourner in a foreign land'" [Exod 2:22]). The paradigmatic story makes the child alternately the child of Fate and Fortune; the Hebrew story seems to give the Hebrews themselves a hand in shaping Providence. Moses returns from rustication not to reclaim princely status in Egypt, but to repudiate Egyptian status there altogether, and to attempt to reclaim status not for himself, but for Israel: he is born in exile, and so his "home" is paradoxically revealed as being "abroad". Moses' story keeps disturbing the paradigm, and yet the paradigm keeps echoing through the story, perhaps in part because we have heard another version of it before. This is the almost equally non-conforming version of the story of Joseph. The initiative of Joseph anticipates that of the Mosaic ministry, for Joseph is the son of Jacob who went out seeking for his brothers (Gen 37:16).

Joseph is highborn, but only by tribal standards (as the first son of his father's most honored wife); he is given a recognition-token of his status (his coat). He is rejected, not as a child by his parent, but as a young man by his wicked step-brothers. They in effect expose him to die, and bring back the report of the death of the "child" (again within the convention). Here Judah or Reuben or the satyr-like Ishmaelites have the preservative role that in the Moses story falls to Moses' sister. Preserved abroad and rising to honors, Joseph does not eventually return to his home, but he does return his family to him, and is recognized and vindicated. It seems, then, that each Biblical story exhibits about half of the paradigm, complementarily distributed. And again the Egyptian/Hebrew dialectic is present, not only in each character, but between the two of them. Joseph is a Hebrew who assimilates with Egypt and becomes "father to Pharaoh"; he calls the Hebrew into Egypt and, in a series of repeating scenes, confronts and judges over the brothers who formerly disputed his ascendancy - now he stands in the place of Pharaoh and God. Moses is an Egyptianized Hebrew who becomes the reverse, the adopted son of Pharaoh's daughter who alienates himself from the land of his birth, calls the Hebrews out of Egypt - and, in a series of repeating scenes, confronts and judges over Pharaoh on behalf of God and the kinsmen who formerly questioned his authority over them.

Even the store-cities being built with Hebrew labor at the opening of Exodus are a continuation of the seven-year plans instituted by Joseph - Joseph the provider. Joseph is credited, moreover, with creating the monopolistic unity of Egypt under Pharaoh; at the same time he sponsors his own family reunion in Egypt, bringing his family towards that re-uniting self-recognition that depends on each brother making himself his brother's keeper, that is, his redeemer or bondsman. Moses rejects the monopoly of force enjoyed by the imperial state, even as he brings his own people to form a communion recognizing the world-sovereignty of God and their indebtedness to Him for their redemption from bondage.[3]

The Patriarchal narrative is a saga, or "on-going" story, the continuing saga of God's covenanting through three generations with the line descending from Abraham. The Joseph story is a small novel, and what is novel in it, and an innovation in the Patriarchal serial, is the sense of mutual obligations binding the individual member of the family or tribe to securing the welfare of his fellow-members. Without this foundation neither the Mosaic understanding of the covenant nor the Mosaic legislating of social concern (and more especially the welfare legislation) would be possible. (Moses' defense of the Midianite daughters at the well [Exod 2:16-22], an exemplary episode in the "pre-ministry" of

Moses, anticipates this legislating of responsibility.)

As many have seen, Moses' exile from Egypt in Midian stands not only <u>before</u> Moses' repatriation to "Israel", but <u>in place of it</u>. Moses' sojourning in the pastoral world of Midian prefigures Israel's future in the wilderness using story-elements drawn from the Patriarchal past. Both the betrothal-encounter at the well and the vocational theophany at the burning bush are recognizably Patriarchal, the latter explicitly so. But unlike the Patriarch, Moses does not meet at the well a wife to whom the future husband is virtually pre-contracted by kinship ties. And Moses is not invited home by the daughters because this is how betrothal arrangements are to be managed (the skillful character at the well - Rebekah, Jacob - proves the stronger in other encounters and matches). No, Moses helps the daughters at the well not because he desires one of them for a wife (like Jacob helping Rachel [Genesis 29]), but because Moses is a <u>stranger</u> among them. And yet we have a trustworthy feeling that we are back among the pieties of the Patriarchal world, and that Moses has found a "home" or a "house" in Midian not to be found in Egypt.

Joseph also returns home in a prefigurative way. All the Hebrews in Egypt carry the corpse of Jacob up to the Promised Land, in a proto-exodus carefully placed at the end of Genesis. Similarly, in the actual exodus, the Israelites leaving Egypt take with them the embalmed - or Egyptianized - corpse of Joseph with them. These two actions, taken together, symbolically assert the continuity of the story of Mosaic Israel with the Patriarchal saga and its innovative Josephic sequel.

So far we have viewed the Mosaic life story in terms of the antecedant story of Joseph. But the story of Moses has other parallels in the story of Israel that follows. It is as though the story of his life has been assimilated to the national religious "history" of Israel.

Moses is born in Egypt, where he seeks to intervene for his countrymen there	Israel finds itself in Egypt, where it is ministered to byMoses, who intervenes intervenes with Pharaoh
Moses departs from Egypt as a fugitive	Israel departs from Egypt in haste, or is expelled
Moses sojourns with the priest in Midian	Israel wanders with Moses and Aaron in the wilderness

Moses is called by God at the mountain of God	Israel is called by God at the mountain of God
Moses parts from his father-in-law in Midian	Israel parts from Moses' father-in-law after covenanting with God at Sinai
Moses returns to rejoin "Israel" and to intervene with Pharaoh on Israel's behalf	Israel sets out from Sinai to return to the land of Israel after Moses intervenes with God on its behalf
Moses works signs before Pharaoh and precedes to plagues culminating in the death of Egypt's first-born	Israel is plagued by God for bad faith and is ultimately destroyed by God in the form of the elder generation
Moses and Israel enter on the wilderness before the Red Sea, and pass through the Red Sea where Pharaoh and his captains and his army all die	Israel leaves the wilderness and passes through enemy territories unharmed and undefeated, and enters the Trans-Jordan where Moses confirms Joshua captain of Israel and dies
Moses and Israel enter on the wilderness beyond the Red Sea, where God feeds his people on manna	Israel crosses the Jordan and enters a land flowing with milk and honey

According to this parallel, Moses' earlier life establishes a paradigm for the exodus itself, and for the subsequent life of Mosaic Israel. It was in the mountain that it was revealed to Moses that he was to return to the Israel in Egypt, and that this Israel would return to the mountain and to the territorial Israel. Thus this pattern is one more of the prescriptive paradigms that God shows Moses in the mountain.

Moses shares the life of his people, and shares his life with them. His life is converted, as it were, into Israel's, while Israel's is converted to that of Moses. Moses, as it were, pre-participates in the life of Israel, even as Israel symbolically repossesses the life of Moses.

Confessional texts show us that both later generations and individual Israelites not only believed in the redeeming power of the exodus, but also in the sustaining power of the wilderness-experience (Exod 15:22 - Numbers 36). Surely there was a sense in Israel that during this time Israel possessed an enhanced consciousness of itself, both as a lost and found generation and as an isolated and communal self. For what the wilderness experience amounts to is a prolonged version of an initiatory "rite de passage", or life-crisis ritual.[4] Like Moses in Midian, the Hebrews are a "liminal community", that is, a group of neophytes temporarily deprived of the status and support of the more established society that they are on the threshold of joining; they exist peripherally and in a critical polarity to that society, in a "limbo" of the virtually pre-existent. Vulnerable and afraid, shrouded from public view, thrown upon the mercy of their guides and the voice of one beyond them, they live in fear of their lives (for it is their lives that are in doubt), exceptionally dependent and in need of exceptional care and succour and graciousness. The conditions of this un-covenanted state are well described in Ezek 16:4-7, where the metaphor is of a post-natal and post-partum isolation:

> And as for your birth, on the day you were born your navel string was not cut, nor were you washed with water to cleanse you, nor rubbed with salt, nor swathed with bands. No eye pitied you, to do any of these things to you out of compassion for you, but you were cast out on the open field, for you were abhorred, on the day that you were born. And when I passed by you, and saw you weltering in your blood, I said to you in your blood, "live", and I made you a myriad like a plant of the field. And you grew up and became tall and arrived at full maidenhood; your breasts were formed, and your hair had grown; yet you were naked and bare.

Comparing the Israelites in the wilderness to Moses in Midian suggests that the wilderness texts describe the introversion, sequestration, and quarantine of a corporate personality betaking itself into the uncultivated wastes to discover the patterns that are to govern its subsequent nationally-bound existence.

The wilderness period is an expanded threshold between two spaces, or a threshold that itself has widened to become a space in its own right, with two thresholds of its own. These are the thresholds marked by one generation's going out (into the wilderness), and another generation's going in (out of the wilderness into the Promised Land). If the movement across this threshold constituted but one momentum (as the parallelism of Ps 106:9 might hint: "He rebuked the Red Sea, and it became dry; and he led them through the deep as through a desert"), there would be no buffer-space but rather a bridge across chaos. Instead, the narrative offers by contrast various objections to such an advance, whether these objections are generated by considerations of military strategy, or by hesitations upon the threshold which are punished by wandering or abiding there. In some way Israel was qualified for the Promised Land by the wilderness, either penally, or through trial, or by service to God.

Into the threshold-space of wilderness the authors of the Pentateuch have interpolated the whole of the Mosaic legislation, thus confirming its enlargement both theologically and textually. The narrative itself anticipates this development at the outset, for it shows us a miniature expansion of the wilderness tradition upon its very threshold - a doubling of the threshold - through Moses' doubling back and camping along the Egyptians side of the Red Sea, in its "wilderness" (Exod 13:18). Moses' delay here is divinely inspired, and seems to anticipate the future dilation of the wilderness texts and narratives. Apparently Israel's encampments by the Sea provoke Pharaoh's pursuit, by keeping Israel within the range of Egypt. But this very jeopardizing of Israel's escape, while it seems to cooperate with an enemy that seeks to captian Israel back to Egypt, is instrumental in securing Israel's final emancipation from Egypt, for it leads to the swallowing up of Pharaoh and his troops. (The swallowing up prefigures the swallowing up of the evil generation in the wilderness, and the swallowing up of Dathan and Abiram in terms that echo those of the Red Sea [Num 16:1-35].) Simlarly, God's decree that the people tarry in the wilderness (Num 14:20-25) may appear both a concession to their cry to appoint another captain to take them back to Egypt, and a positive step towards the eventual crossing of the threshold by a new and purged generation.

The term "captain" is important here, for it occurs immediately after the appointment of Joshua, who has just been ordained (by being renamed [Num 13:8,16]) to conduct the abortive reconnaissance mission (Numbers 13-14). The texts associate the wilderness sojourning with the migratory patterns and seasonal nomadism of pastoralists, who enter pastureland annually, only to return, at the end of the season, to the wilderness where some fodder survives through the winter. Thus the seasonal circling of the shepherd is in some ways opposed to the kind of campaign leadership provided by the captain, who takes the land shared with agriculturalists for his own, rather than merely being a seasonal guest or sojourner in that land. Now Moses uses the term "shepherd" when he appoints Joshua as a leader for the people who will "go out before them and come in before them, who shall lead them out and bring them in" (Num 27:16-17). But such an office really supersedes that of shepherd, and that of Moses. The appointment answers the charge of Dathan and Abiram, the charge, essentially, that Moses is no captain: he has really only led Israel on a kind of retreat from the Promised Land, not into the land flowing with mild and honey, but out of it (Num 16:13). Moses is more truly the shepherd, circling through the land of agriculturalists, and out of it again. Joshua is the spearhead of advance, but Moses is like the buffer-space we have described: constituted out of the more nomadic motions of advance and retreat, isolated between the thresholds of a definitive out and definitive in.

The Genesis of the Exodus

I

To Moses (the Moses who survives in the texts, the Moses of faith) Israel attributed the genesis of her national existence. But Israel is also in the line of the Patriarchs, and the Patriarchs are in the line of the Creation, and therefore such an Israel also exists - as deutero-Isaiah makes clear - from the foundation of the world. Exodus and Creation belong together. That is why, in the story of how Israel was finally and definitively set apart from her Egyptian pursuers, that the parting of the Red Sea opens on the primeval abyss, even while revealing the original dry land and the foundation of the firmament (with Exod 14:21b; 15:8, compare Isa 51:9b-10; Gen 1:2,6,9; also Num 16:30).

It is Pharaoh who is finally "exposed" on the waters, destroyed by God as the water-monster Tiamat is destroyed by Marduk:

> Sheol is naked before God, and Abaddon has no covering. He stretches out the north over the void, and hangs the earth upon nothing. He binds up the waters in his thick clouds, and the cloud is not rent under them....By his power he stilled the sea; by his understanding he smote Rahab. By his wind the heavens were made fair; his hand pierced the fleeing serpent. (Job 26:6-8, 12-13)

It is to such a one that Moses owes his power to still or imprison water (the first plague Moses causes is a plague of thirst) and his power to release it from captivity (Tiamat had absorbed all world's water). As God smote Rahab and pierced the fleeing serpent, so Moses struck the Nile and the rock (Exod 7:20; 17:5-6; Num 20:11; Ps 78:20) and confounded the fleeing Pharaoh (Exod 14:25-28). The heavens were made by the word of the Lord and the breath of his mouth, when he gathered the waters together in a heap - so Ps 33:6-7. According to Ps 78:13 and the Exodus accounts, the waters of the Red Sea were stood up in a heap, and according to Ps 106:9 the waters were stayed at the Lord's rebuke, that is, at his word. This rebuke is implied by the primeval stilling of the seas, as in Ps 89:9-11, which links the stilling of the seas with the dividing of Rahab, the scattering of enemies, and the founding of the world. Similarly, the primeval waters stood above the mountains and fled at the Creator's rebuke, at the laying of the beams of his creation in the waters and the covering of the foundations of the earth with the deep, in Ps 104:3,5-7; and they are bound that they may not again cover the earth (v 9). We may conclude that Pharaoh perished in a version of the Flood.

Exod 15:16 speaks of the stilling of the peoples who are Israel's enemies, by their wonder at the Red Sea event, but this motif is otherwise turned on Israel, Israel's murmering itself being subject to rebuke: "The Lord said to Moses, 'Why do you cry to me?'" (Exod 14:15); "Moses said to the people, '...you have only to be still'" (Exod 14:13-14). As these rebukes and silencings show, the Red Sea event, like the Creation event, came to be understood as the work of the word, a deutero-word of Creation addressed to the waters. The most important text is Ps 18:15-16:

> Then the channels of the sea were seen,
>   and the foundations of the world were laid bare,
> at thy rebuke, O Lord,
>   at the blast of the breath of thy nostrils.
> He reached me from on high, he took me,
>   he drew me out of many waters.

The drawing of the delivered party out of the waters, of course, invokes the etymology of Moses' name, as does a parallel recollection in Isa 63:11-13a:

> Then he remembered the days of old,
>   of Moses his servant.

45

Where is he who brought up out of the sea
    the shepherds of his flock?
Where is he who put in the midst of them
    his holy Spirit [i.e. the blast of his nostrils?],
who caused his glorious arm
    to go at the right hand of Moses,
who divided the waters before them
    to make for himself an everlasting name,
who led them through the depths?

Here it is the shepherds themselves who are saved out of the waters. More typically, as in Ps 77:16-20 (where the waters are afraid of the wonder-working God and the earth trembles at the voice of his thunder), the shepherds are the saviors - though an invisible Savior walks before them (vv 19-20):

Thy way was through the sea,
    thy path through the great waters;
    yet thy footprints were unseen.
Thou didst lead thy people like a flock
    by the hand of Moses and Aaron.

We can see from these texts, because of the resemblance to the birth-legend of Moses, that Israel, in being drawn from the waters, is being born. We can also see that it is Moses' calling to draw Israel out and to interpret for it its emergence. This virtually maieutic function aligns Moses' vocation with the profession of the midwives (Exod 1:15-22). Otto Rank, who studied the myth of the birth of the hero, also drew attention to birth-trauma, a shock that the Song at the Sea records from the point of view of things to come: "The peoples have heard, they tremble; pangs (ḥîl; cf. Jer 50:43: "pain [ḥîl] as of a woman in travail"; Jer 50:43) have seized on the inhabitants of Philistia....Terror and dread fall upon them...they are still as stone,...till the people pass by whom thou has purchased" (Exod 15:14,16). Somewhat similarly, there is a great cry throughout Egypt on the night of the sparing of Israel's first-born (Exod 11:6; 12:30). This cry must match the crying out of the people under Pharaoh's oppression, and that cry is carefully repeated at the shore of the Red Sea (Exod 14:10). Neh 9:9 brings out the parallel: "thou didst see the affliction of our fathers in Egypt and hear their cry at the Red Sea ". Between the crying out of Israel and the crying out of Egypt we seem to come upon an obstetrical interpretation of the exodus. We may compare the following from Paul (Rom 8:18-24):

I consider that the sufferings of this present time are not worth comparing with the glory that is to be revealed to us. For the creation waits with eager longing for the revealing of the sons of God; for the creation was subjected to futility, not of its own will but by the will of him who subjected it in hope; because the creation itself will be set free from its bondage to decay and obtain the glorious liberty of the children of God. We know that the whole creation has been groaning in travail until now; and not only the creation, but we ourselves, who have the first fruits of the Spirit, groan inwardly as we wait for adoption as sons, the redemption of our bodies. For this hope we were saved.

It is possible to consider this Pauline text to be a searching homily upon the meaning of the exodus-deliverance itself.

II

The Red Sea event suggests the creation and birth of Israel. The same event is a crucial datum in Israel's coming-to-consciousness. Paradoxically, this birth of consciousness is discernable in precisely the charge that Israel forgot the mighty acts of the Lord in Egypt, even before the people were delivered at the Red Sea (Ps 106:7), before it was divided (Ps 78:11-13), or else in the wilderness (Ps 78:42-44). Both of the Psalms in question are histories of Israel's forgetfulness, and so it is not surprising that they find their subject everywhere. Nonetheless, these texts suggest that Moses has a role in bridging a void in Israel's historical explanation of itself: a void between a legendary pre-Israel of the Patriarchs and the covenanted Israel of the tribal league; a void between a stateless class of itinerant servants called Hebrews and a people who had incorporated as the servant of God; and a void between an Israel in which each man was his own priest and an Israel in which the whole elect nation was thought of as an answerable moral subject. We owe our portrait of Moses to Israel's grateful sense that somehow it had traversed this void, entering with him on the limbo-space of the wilderness: a space of pre-existence between non-entity in Egypt and identity in Israel, between vassalage in foreign lands and installation in her own sovereign space. Navigating the threshold over which Israel passes into historical existence, Moses finally becomes part of this threshold, at the borders of the Promised Land.

On these borders the Moses who commissions Joshua to

succeed him is somewhat like the trans-Jordanian tribes who lead the entry into the Promised Land, only to return from it to their pre-occupation settlements upon its frontier. Their retreat brings to mind the failure of the earlier generation to possess the Promised Land without tarrying in the wilderness (Num 32:8-13). This return to the frontier exhibits what we might term a "structure of recall", a structure which underlies the Red Sea narration, where, the calling forth from Egypt is told in counterpoint with re-calling precedent events in Egypt.

The place of the Red Sea in this structure of recall is particularly emphasized by a doubling-back in the narrative itself. The vigil-night of Passover (Exod 12:1-13) doubles back to the three days of the plague of darkness, when Israel alone had light and was invisible to Egypt (Exod 10:22-23). The destruction of Pharaoh's army in turn recalls the destruction of Pharaoh's first-born on the night of Israel's being passed over (Exod 14:27-28; 13:29-30). And the wilderness sojourn, during which Israel's cult was instituted prior to entry into the Promised Land, doubles back to the delay, in entering the wilderness proper, upon the shores of the Red Sea (Exod 14:1-4). Thus each of these events duplicates the next. For the three nights of the darkness-plague are a "little wilderness" (or a pre-wilderness) themselves: that is, an absenting of Israel from Egypt, during which Israel enjoys divinely provided light, just as it subsequently is protected in the wilderness by the pillar of fire by night (Exod 13: 21-22). Now when Pharaoh asked who the Lord was, Moses and Aaron told him that he was one who required of them a three days' journey into the wilderness to sacrifice - lest he fall upon them with pestilence and sword (Exod 5:3 - and indeed, both plague and sword fall upon Israel at the very consecrating of the levitical priesthood at Sinai). If the plague of darkness stands in place of that three days' journey, then not simply the Sinai events, but the Passover itself is the scheduled sacrifice; it is both plague and sword to those who are not making it. But an analogous toll is taken on the manhood of Egypt at the Red Sea, and it is thus significant that the rout is preceded by two nights' worth of encampments in the Red Sea wilderness. On the third day God wins the kind of victory that Israel was elsewhere to dignify with the name of sacrifice.

We may conclude that if Israel forgot all that God had done for it by the time of the Red Sea (Ps 106:7; 78:11-13), it was not for want of reiteration and recapitulation. But the imputation in these two Psalms in fact belongs to a convention, the convention of superimposing the origins of a history upon a lapse in consciousness: for every beginning is an ending, and so a break with the continuity of memory. Thus forgetting and remembering fold into one another as the story is told. Four generations intervene between "Jacob" and Mosaic Israel, the number of generations to which God will remember to be gracious (Exod 33:19). The same God did not forget Joseph, but caused him to forget his father's house (Gen 40:23; 41:9,51). The God of Exodus remembered his covenant with the three generations of patriarchs (Exod 2:24) in a passage that follows hard upon the naming of Joseph's son Manasseh, "making-to-forget".

Thus of the many ways of beginning the story of exodus, we may single out a particular lapse of consciousness: the ignorance of Pharaoh who knew not Joseph (Exod 1:8). We may compare as a beginning the generation that arose "who did not know the Lord or the work which he had done for Israel" after the death of Joshua's generation - so begins the history of the Judges (Judg 2:10b). The scarcity of word and vision at the time of the call of Samuel (1 Sam 3:1b) has a similar function in the history of the kingship.

Another convention is at work here also, the convention of an evil-minded generation that is itself condemned to perish, even as those surviving that generation find their way back to Yahweh - for the knowledge of God survives and is transmitted to the present somehow. The convention first appears in the Flood story, where the oblivious generation is doomed to oblivion. Now Moses, while not a "righteous survivor" like Noah, is nonetheless the moral leader who brings the sanctified stock through the waters. Moses is like Noah in leaving behind him not only Egypt but the obscurity of the past - in the case of the Flood, the point beyond which what happened in history cannot be traced. Thus it is appropriate that the hero of the threshold of Israel's historical-national consciousness himself be borne into the Egyptian status (from which he will return to Israel) in an ark on the water. Moses' being drawn out of the water could be said to indicate the obscurity of origins - of Moses himself and of Israel.

And yet Moses is also the flood-crossing hero, who escapes across the frontier, or the barrier to any deeper penetration backward in time, with his memory intact. For before Egypt there lies the Patriarchal story, and the call-story of Moses (Exodus 3) credits him with reviving the memory of the divine protection enjoyed by the fathers of old. As we have shown, there are reasons to think of the Joseph story as having a purposeful post-Patriarchal and pre-Mosaic narrative position in the Canon, which supplies a Mosaic "antetype" and so links the Patriarchal narrative to the Mosaic one. Such a literary device is also imitative of the keeping and transmitting of history:[5] the attempt to bring a past story up to date, and to bring the present back to its beginnings.

III

As a representation of the origins of Israel, we have seen the exodus as governed by a metaphor of creation which is also a metaphor of birth, and a metaphor of coming to consciousness which is also a metaphor of recalling. A third way of understanding the originary force of the exodus begins with the motifs of genocide and preservation, from which the story itself also begins. We may again invoke the story of the evil Noachic generation. It was destroyed for its violence and evil, but the obscurely interpolated story of the giants seems also to be directed against a population explosion and against longevity. Apparently these were forms of evil gigantism too. Thus the Flood story as a whole begins from the multiplication of men, and shortly finds Yahweh resolving to limit the human life-span (Gen 6:1,3). This hint of a jealous program of population control appears before the Flood proper, just as the genocidal motif appears before the specific endangering and rescue of Moses by means of the waters.

Pharaoh's attempt to destroy the very generation of Hebrews that he has enslaved makes very little economic sense, and must be attributed to pure animosity or viewed as a metaphor for the cheapening of life through slavery. But in practice slaves are cheaper the more there are of them, and the slave-owner will be the wealthier the more his property breeds - and if he were to breed selectively, he ought to kill off the females, not the males. Still, while we cannot really rationalize the link of infanticide and enslavement, we could make sense of either one as an attempt to bridle numerical increase. We might compare the recruitment of slaves with the taking of a census that serves the purposes of conscription. In terms of the "Creation" parallel from Genesis, the imperial ruler is a kind of creator manqué, attempting to rationalize his used or useless subjects, and so impose his kind of order on potential chaos. But in terms of another parallel, Pharaoh's inspiration might be considered demonic: "Satan stood up against Israel, and incited David to number Israel. So David said to Joab and his commanders of his army, 'Go number Israel...'" (1 Chron 21:1-2). The same story in 2 Samuel 24 ends with David given a choice of punishment by a prophet. Significantly for our theme, David chooses to subject Israel directly to the punishment of God, three days of plague. Plague is one of the forms in which the Lord "visits" or "numbers" his people (cf. pāqad ["visit"] in Num 16:20 with the plagues in vv 35,46-50).

Thus as metaphors for beginnings, increase and its assessment, tend to be opposed, each checking the other. Large numbers result in an attempt to terminate their growth; assessment brings a plague on the people of the assessor. We may compare the generous plenitude celebrated in the Table of Nations (Genesis 10) with the monopolistic unity plagued with confusion at the Tower of Babel (Genesis 11). Nothing is very clear here, but numbers apparently have a negative, unclean, swarming and epidemic form, and a positive, sanctified, prolific form. Similarly, numbering has either sinister or affirmative effect. Moses is told to number Israel for war at the opening of Numbers, the initial sense being positive; and yet the census must be taken again, for the death of a whole generation in the wilderness intervenes (the first die by plague), and not a man numbered originally remains (Num 26:64-65). The census of Caesar Augustus in the gospel is similarly positive, for it is ecumenical - and similarly negative, for it is part of the levying of a tax.

The creation-narratives in Genesis also suggest this double, positive-negative way of beginning. In the positive narrative, man is ceded world-sovereignty and told to increase and multiply. In the negative narrative man falls into labor and the Lord says he will greatly multiply the woman's pain in child-bearing. God's purposes and Pharaoh's are roughly opposed according to these two acounts. Increase and its containment also furnish the grounds for a kind of parabolic narration about the impositions of an ascendant bureaucracy: taxation, military conscription, and forced labor. In the historical period, of course, forced labor was not the peculiar imposition of Egypt on Israel; it was the imposition of the kingship of Solomon (1 Kgs 9:15-24; 11:26-29), who multiplied horses, wives, treasures, and works (Deut 17:16-18).

By seeing Pharaoh's programs as a form of resistance to the Creator, or as a usurpation of his prerogatives, we can also see their relation to the program of the Creator himself, in the plague-narrative. For Pharaoh basically considers the

Hebrews to be a plague: they were many in the land, and the plagues are on, over, and throughout the land. Egypt is punished by a nightmare in the very shape of Pharaoh's anxieties, by epidemics of uncontrollable numbers and by a vast uncleanness that has everything spilling and swarming out of its proper category and ratio and number.[6] Besides this punishment of Pharaoh's attempt to limit nature at the mouth of the womb, there is also the Creator's punishment of the empire-building of a rival. The plagues offer God's critique of the universal slave-state, with its atomization of the human community, its production schedules and quotas and shortages of raw materials, and its systematizing of its labor force into uniform building-blocks even while treating its human raw materials like stubble and vermin. Pharaoh's schemes are a parody of state-planning - the "store cities" presumably anticipate shortages - for Pharaoh alleges a threat that he sets about bringing into existence. The threat he anticipates is that danger posed by a dispossessed class, and his delusion is that the way to avoid trouble is to stir it up. Pharaoh seems dimly to know that his shrewdness is creating the very problem he thinks to avoid; what he does not know is that he is fulfilling the terms of a larger plan, variously announced in Genesis (to Jacob at 46:3, by Joseph at 50:20), and in addition creating the future unity of Israel by making it a class. Pharaoh's daughter is conscripted by the same plan, for she is inveigled into temporarily offering her protection to the future leader of this class. Even the midwives are able to take advantage of Pharaoh, for the lie they tell him - that the Hebrew women bear virtually spontaneously - is just the lie his edict shows him readiest to believe. However ironic, we may call this lie the annunciation to Pharaoh.

Although one may speak of Pharaoh's initiative as genocidal, this motif is really only the shadow cast backwards over the people by Pharaoh's enmity to Moses. The hereditary leader who disregards his own people's trouble is opposed to the unborn leader who "sees" and heeds the cry of this people for deliverance. Pharaoh's murderousness towards Hebrew males finds raison d'être with the threat of extinction to the infant Moses. Pharaoh's impulse is not genocidal if by this we mean the systematic liquidation of a truly distinctive group which becomes the object of such attention by being (in Hegelian-Marxist terms) the alienated essense of established society. Only Moses finally furnishes Egypt with such an object. The Hebrews are no such scapegoat, as Moses virtually tells us when he says the Hebrews might become the object of retaliation if they carried out their sacrifices in Egypt. This anxiety betrays the fact that to date the Hebrews have no cult (they are going out into the wilderness to get one). Thus the kind of anti-semitism that battens on a repugnance for some allegedly sinister content of Jewish rites does not yet exist. We may compare and contrast the situation of the Jews in Babylon in the Book of Esther. Like the exodus, the events of that story become the pre-text for a religious holiday. But the Jews are already religiously differentiated from the Babylonians, for they will not worship the king; and they already have a well-placed leader, for Mordecai is the "father" of the new queen, who is herself Jewish. Moses, on the other hand, is the "son" of the Princess, but as his infant status tells us, the Hebrews do not have enough of a political identity to have a leader. Thus Pharaoh's attempt on the life of the unborn Moses falls into place as an attempt to prevent the Hebrews from begetting one. Pharaoh's precaution proves a self-fulfilling prophecy (the characteristic effect of the paranoid point of view), and thus an instrument of God's continuing providence - Pharaoh's midwives might say, with Joseph, "God sent me before you to preserve for you a remnant on earth" and "God meant it for good, to bring it about that many people should be kept alive" (Gen 45:7; 50:20). For the increased pressure on the Hebrews pre-unionizes them and readies them for a new, divinely inspired leader.

IV

The same social pressure, climaxing in the expulsion from Egypt, forms the Hebrew's first rite, the Passover. Circumcision might be thought to be the prior rite, since it has patriarchal patronage (Genesis 17), and since Moses is subjected to a version of it on his return from Midian (Exod 4:24-27). It thus belongs to our wilderness theme, and certainly the wilderness period proper will constitute a circumcision of the tribe. The Mosaic version is also patriarchal because the flint that Zipporah uses at Exod 4:24-27 combines the fire and knife that Abraham carries with him to the sacrifice of Isaac (Gen 22:6-7). The sacrifice of Isaac leads to a renewal of God's covenant with Abraham, which is otherwise, in Genesis 17, accepted through circumcision. In other words, the covenant, the displaced sacrifice and circumcision all imply a sparing of Abraham's seed. But the Mosaic version of circumcision reveals a deeper analogy between the rite and the substitute for the sacrifice of the first born: it reveals that the rite, like the sacrifice of Isaac, has the character of a divine passing over - a sparing of life secured by the shedding of blood. For the prime datum of the Mosaic version is that of a divine nocturnal visitation. Thus the story is placed directly after God's threat to Pharaoh's first-born son (Exod4:23). In the Patriarchal narrative, circumcision belongs to the father's bequest to the son, and it is a racial kind of inheritance. In the Mosaic narrative, circumcision is more the token of admission to the cultic community. Moses' own sparing by a rite of circumcision resembles the sparing of the Hebrew houses on the night of Passover, and so Passover itself is the Mosaic circumcision: the circumcision of the tribe.

Before the sparing of Israel on this night, it was not quite possible for Israel to be a scapegoat in Egypt. This condition is reversed by the instituting of the Passover, even as the passing of the angel through Egypt offers the people the means to escape the situation which their new distinctiveness has created. Moses makes his God responsible for the disasters plaguing Egypt and thus gives the Egyptians cause to expel his people into the desert. Such an expulsion is the logical alternative to the earlier program of genocide. The Passover, however, features symbols of both alternatives: the unleavened bread symbolizing preparations for an unprepared departure, and the sacrificial lamb symbolizing the blood that was shed to mark the places where no life was to be taken. We may compare the scapegoat ritual, where one animal is driven into the wilderness to meet a numen (spirit), and the other is sacrificed for sin. Of course the Hebrews are not sacrificed, but their first-born are sanctified. And the Egyptian first-born are not sacrificed, but their first-born are killed.

Although Pharaoh's son is merely taken in the general plague, there are hints in God's original announcement in Exod 4:23 that this son is an object from the start. If so, then perhaps the shadow of other takings of the life of a king's son fall across the sequence of events: foundation-sacrifices make at the founding of a city, and appeasement-sacrifices make in desperate straits, as the city is about to fall (cf. 2 Kgs 3:26-27). But it is just such a son's life that Israel, like Abraham at the sacrifice of Isaac, is given back. The gift anticipates, however obscurely, the emptiness of the sepulchre built for the King's Son in the New Testament - a son once upon a time called out of Egypt.

We may now ask why God chooses this form for plaguing the Egyptians, or rather for sparing the Hebrews. For we are told that "against any of the people of Israel not a dog shall growl" (Exod 11:7), which suggests that what they are spared is a pogrom. Why else the atmosphere of a sinister human visitation, the vigil behind marked doors, and the angel of destruction - or company of angels (in Ps 78:49)? As strangers in Egypt, the Hebrews recall Lot trapped in Sodom, provided with guardian angels yet pressured into offering up his daughters to potentially fatal abuse (Gen 19:1-10; cf. Judg 19:16-28). Like the Hebrews as instructed by God, Lot is offering a semi-sacred meal just before the evil visit - for he is hosting the sacred strangers. Now the Passover meal is definitely restricted to Israel, and significantly in terms of the circumcision. Strangers, however, are welcome to it, if they have been circumcised (Exod 12:43-49), if, that is, they have been included in what appears, from Moses' symbolic circumcision, to be a community of blood. The sign in the flesh includes one in this community - with which we must contrast the apotropaic effect of the sign on the door, which excludes, and which is also a sign made with blood. This is the blood of a sacrifice eaten within the house - and since it spares those within the house, the sacrifice must stand in place of the deaths of the Egyptian first-born. Thus the Hebrew cult is generated by the consecration of Israel's first-born and the divine violence directed against Pharaoh's first-born. Although it is unmarked houses that are not protected, one can imagine other circumstances in which the marked houses would also be the proscribed ones - or, in time of plague, the quarantined ones. In any case, this is how Pharaoh would have staged the purge of the Hebrews if it were a purely political one. Thus the Hebrews arrive at ceremonial religion at the same time that they acquire an identity sufficient to sanction genocidal violence against them. And yet the sign of blood excludes this violence, even as it displaces from the Hebrews to the Egyptians what might be once again described as a circumcision of the tribe, the taking of a part for the whole.

Pharaoh's shrewdness creates the Hebrew leadership: that is the effect of his very enterprise in purging it from the womb. Similarly, God creates the religious consciousness of Israel through exposing Israel to the terrible scrutiny of the angel of destruction. The pogrom visited upon the Egyptian majority is something of a pre-emptive strike on God's part, since the logic of scapegoatism typically makes the stranger in society's midst guilty of the disasters engulfing the community. Moses himself has said that if the Hebrews offered sacrifice in Egypt they would be stoned as foreigners, and indeed that is how they are expelled: they are said to be going to be driven out.

One thinks of a suggestive episode in the movie version of a modern Italian novel by Giorgio Bassani, The Garden of the Finzi-Continis. A Jewish family, celebrating Passover in an increasingly Fascist Italy, has their service interrupted first once and then again by the ringing of the telephone: when the call is answered the calling party has hung up. Clearly the call is a kind of anonymous threat of violent interruption - it is a threat because it is in the character of ceremonies that they not be interrupted. And yet all sacrifice consecrates the interruption of a life. The tragedy of Jewish identity has been that historically it is a Passover interrupted by a pogrom. The triumph of Israel's identity is that it is formed around an occasion that contains the polar terms in a symbiotic whole. Passover consecrates an interruption in the life of the celebrating community, and incorporates that interruption into its celebrations, surrounding it with a set-apart time and making it holy. Passover is instituted upon - and is the constituting of - an interruption.

The Constituting of an Interruption

Like the Passover, Moses' own life is the constituting of an interruption. It bridges the very gap he creates by putting Egypt behind him and Israel in front of him. The symbol of his life is found in the threshold he mediates. His role is created dialectically, as a twice-alienated Hebrew who dies outside of Israel, or as an honorary but excommunicated Egyptian. He is presented in this way not in spite of his appointment to be the great raiser of the consciousness of Israel, but because of it. Only such a "subject", coming from outside Israel, could make Israel his "object": and so the servant of God, rather than the slave of Pharaoh. The way from the deliverance from Egypt and the wilderness to the Holy War is through the Red Sea, but the way from the oblivion of Egypt to the identity of Israel is through Moses. Through Moses passes the consecration of Israel's identity to God, the corporation of priests and holy men inside Israel being founded by Moses from beyond it. Through Moses passes the identification of Israel with Israel's borders, and thus its identification with itself rather than Moses. Moses' own borderline situation is reflected in his situation near the end of the Book of

56

Numbers, where he is prescribing the boundaries of the people's inheritance within the Promised Land. He stands upon the boundary he will not cross, giving Mosaic endorsement to borders he will scarcely see. Tribally a Levite, he prescribes the landless levitical inheritance, and appoints the priestly cities of refuge, from the standpoint of his own, deeper disqualification from inheriting in Israel.

What does it mean for the larger process of the Bible, that Moses did not enter the Promised Land? Surely it means that Mosaic Israel had never quite been realized in history, or that its supercession was a foregone conclusion. Mosaic Israel was "somewhere else": in the wilderness, with Moses; in the future, with a military savior; in the past, before the coming of the State. And yet, only with the coming of the State, in the time of David, did Israel expand from within to secure the borders that the storied Moses reached and defined from without. It was presumably from the vantage-point provided by the monarchy that Israel was able to review and summarize its traditional history as a series of backdrops lifting on the present actualization of Israel, and so visualize Moses foreseeing Israel's future inheritance from the peak outside of it. But according to 1 Samuel 8, it was just when Israel adopted the kingship that it gave up the Mosaic kingship of God. We must conclude that the Mosaic inheritance and the Davidic one are equally problematic: we might almost say, equally uninheritable. For the Israelite could see where he had walked up and down the land with sojourning Abraham, but he was no longer a sojourner. He could survey his part of the original creation, and with God pronounce it good; but his sovereignty was passing to the Solomonic bureaucracy. And like the Moses of Deuteronomy, he could begin to cast his Mosaic heritage in closed literary form, and approve of it as a divine fait accompli. But he could also experience that inheritance as a summons beyond him, one that would make him - like another Moses - almost infinitely answerable.

Chapter Four

IN STRANGE WAYS: THE STORY OF SAMSON

John B. Vickery

TO speak of the Old Testament tale of Samson as a short story may, at first sight, appear to be little more than a declaration that as a story it is not long. And yet the more closely we examine it in relation to that literary genre which really only emerged in full-blown form in Europe during the nineteenth century, the more we are struck by two things. The Samson tale, like many others in the Old Testament, stands out as a prototype for certain kinds of later short stories such as those of Bret Harte, Sherwood Anderson, Mark Twain, and William Faulkner, stories that emanate from the sociability of the campfire and related situations and that revolve around the idea of the tall tale in which narrative invention refuses to be shackled by plausibility. At the same time, our knowledge of the short story as a genre and its literary characteristics alerts us to similar traits discernible, at least implicitly, in Old Testament narratives such as that of Samson. As a result of these two perspectives, we come to have a much sharper sense of the ways in which fiction is rooted in the ancient narrative world of folk tale and myth as well as a keener realization of the Old Testament's aspirations to the narrative, structural, and thematic sophistication of technique found in what today we call literature.[1]

When as readers of modern short fiction we turn to Judges 13-16, we find, the more we ponder the tale, several things emerging that in varying degrees break with our expectations. By looking at these more closely, we will see both how the Samson story differs from contemporary stories and also why some of its puzzling or unconventional aspects exist in the form they do. The first and most obvious contrast

58

to the modern short story is the fact of divine intervention in human affairs. At the outset Yahweh's angelic representative appears to Manoah and his wife and on several other occasions Samson is infused unawares with Yahweh's spirit. Thus, the dramatic action of the story as well as the chief character's motivation are inaugurated and maintained by a supernatural power operating outside the ordinary course of events. The effect of this is to establish the divine figure, whose fictive reality is limited to his name, as a pervasive force that shapes the action at the same time as it studies the developing narrative of events. In a word, Yahweh is to the tale's author or authors both its ultimate or primal author and its original audience, while they are but the tale's narrative transmitters.

How far the first part of this phenomenon contrasts with the modern short story is obvious. In the main, the latter, because of the preoccupations of the age and the formal requirements of the genre, is relentlessly secular in character. Violation of natural law by a transcendent agent is scarcely a viable event in twentieth century fiction even in those instances which have an avowedly religious dimension or intent. And when it is introduced, it more likely than not is masked as an accident, as when in J. F. Power's "Morte D'Urban" the descent of grace comes in the form of a stray golf ball striking Father Urban on the head. Nevertheless, the rarity of such divine intervention should not obscure for us the extent to which Yahweh's dual role as author and reader, creator and witness, anticipates one of the most striking features of contemporary fiction. This is its inclination toward what is called self-reflexivity in which, for instance, the telling of the tale becomes the tale's very subject and the real identity of the author becomes a verbal activity of regressive complexity akin to the peeling of an onion in order to arrive at its essential nature. Here the names to set beside the author/editor of Samson are those of Samuel Beckett, Jorge Luis Borges, and John Barth.

A second factor almost as striking as divine intervention is that of the nature of the hero. To say that Samson is an improbable and less than sympathetic figure is to understate the obvious. His physical courage and tribal integrity are beyond question. But his propensity to impulsive, egocentric and arbitrary actions renders him less an admirable human being, a leader around whom men may rally to struggle for justice, independence, and self-redemption than a turbulent, unpredictable and destructive force of nature. In short, he is a kind of folk hero whose exploits arouse not so much the moral approbation of his fellows or of his audience as the awed, incredulous admiration of self-assertive energy run rampant. To this extent he is an anomaly as one of the judges in Israel. As one writer remarks, "his talent would seem to have lain rather in the direction of brawling and fighting, burning down people's corn-ricks, and beating up the quarters of loosewomen; in short, he seems to have shone in the character of a libertine and a rakeshell".[2] His descendants would appear to number, on the physical side, such as Robin Hood, Rob Roy, and Jesse James, and, on the side of shrewd cunning and gleeful duplicity, the amoral rogue of eighteenth century picaresque fiction. What this tells us is that, at least on one level, the dominant concern of the story lies less with the character of the protagonist than with the ingenuity and insouciance of the actions. Samson's behavior is quite literally breathtaking not only in its physical magnitude but also in its calm, bare-faced, moral effrontery. The former drives home to us our perennial fascination with the truly marvellous and incredible in which resides more than a trace of fantasy gratification. The latter, on the other hand, generates, at least incipiently, a mute awe at the man who is alien to social norms and moral sanctions alike, an awe in which the temptation to gratification is tempered by apprehension as to the consequences.

Yet if the protagonist focuses our attention more on his actions than his character, careful readers are also able to detect a significance in the character when viewed in the light of the fact of divine intervention. The issue can perhaps best be joined by way of one critical comment which puts the matter succinctly. The author observes that "as a popular hero Samson needs no explanation; as a charismatic hero he is hard to swallow".[3] Subsequently, this writer goes on to suggest that it is precisely Samson who makes clear what the Israelite notion of this last hero really is: a morally neutral individual no different from other men who becomes the instrument of Yahweh's divine will without any conscious determination of his own. Attractive as this notion may be to an understanding of early Israelite theology, it sounds more than a trifle strange to modern ears, which are accustomed to linking the concept to an ability to inspire both confidence and a willingness to follow loyally. Indeed, one of the most striking things about Samson is precisely the fact that he inspires no confidence in his abilities on the part of others and that he has no followers whatsoever. The men of Judah, for instance, are quick to express their trepidations at his actions against the Philistines and to take active steps to deliver him into his enemy's hands. Thus, if one wishes to describe him as a charismatic hero, that is, one who has received a particular force for power from Yahweh, we have also to keep in mind that, in another sense, he might equally be described as a non-charismatic hero, an individual whose actions engender fear and suspicion together with a manifest reluctance to share in his guerrilla-style attacks on their common enemy and oppressor.

The net effect of this ambivalence concerning Samson's charismatic qualities is to point up and underscore the significance of Yahweh's divine intervention. The opening lines of the Samson story (13:1) set the defining framework for what follows:

> And the people of the Lord again did what was evil in the sight of the Lord; and the Lord gave them into the hand of the Philistines for forty years.

Israel has ignored divine injunctions and prescriptions and so is punished by oppression. Yet it is the same divine figure who embarks on an elaborately circuitous and largely mysterious campaign to defend and free Israel by sending an angel to Manoah and his wife to announce her conception and the ensuing deliverance of Israel by virtue of her son's actions. In short, the dominant weight falls on the role of the divine, not the human, figure. Thus Samson's moral dubiety and non-charismatic aura together testify to the power of the Lord and the mysterious ways in which it is exercised. To be able to invest arbitrarily and at will so unlikely a vehicle with the capacities of physical strength, shrewdness, and, finally, of patience and humble fortitude is irrefutable testimony to the omnipotence and pre-eminence of Yahweh. He takes a bully boy and muscle man bent on the gratification of his own drives and instincts like Samson and makes him the instrument of a nation's defense and rescue as well as the means of authenticating the divinity's power of salvation and therefore his right to be regarded as the true God in contrast to false claimants like Dagon. This provides a sustained and sobering story of the immensity and mysteriousness of the divine agency in human affairs.

Nowhere is the scope and the remoteness of the agency better revealed than in the tale's crashing finale, which shows unmistakably that by the very nature of the case the person touched with temporary incarnation is destined to prove a tragic character. Samson's unexpected and extraordinary actions lead to his eleveation far above ordinary human status and tempt him to reveal secrets connected with the deity. Ultimately, these actions lead - when the divine impulse is mysteriously and enigmatically withdrawn - to emotional and physical humiliation out of which emerges an agonizing kind of self-wisdom (presaging that which must inevitably come from Israel itself) which finally makes possible the tragic fall which is also a transcendence. We see that the whole narrative develops in accord with Yahweh's plan to "deliver Israel from the hand of the Philistines" (13:5), and in the face of that fact the individual vehicle for execution of that plan has an instrumental and illustrative but no personal value. The forces that cluster about Shakespeare's Coriolanus, for instance, and that drive him on to that grimly tragic destiny are the same ones swirling around Samson. The chief difference is that Shakespeare focuses explanatory possibilities on the mysteries of society, family, personality, and their interaction. The author of Judges, on the other hand, concentrates on the more remote mysteries of transcendence, incarnation, and personal and group identity.

Given - the narrative suggests - the facts of divine agency, human accession to spiritual forces, and the parallelism of individual behavior and national fate, it is inevitable and essential that the protagonist assume a tragic role as the final act of the drama of his life. To extend the divine spirit means that it must be withdrawn; to perform superhuman feats entails at some point attendant failures; and to identify an individual hero with a social unit such as a nation indicates that both as erring entities must suffer punishment, the former because he is part of the latter and the nation because it has done evil in the sight of the Lord. The conclusion of the tale captures the twin qualities of hope and grim foreshadowing that this imaginative dialectic embodies. If Samson is the figure of Israel, then it too must face a self-performed casting down and destruction. But by the same token, this linking also entails ultimate deliverance since the children of Israel are consigned to Philistine bondage for a period of forty years and yet Samson "judged Israel twenty years" (16:31). In short, the end is not yet. Samson dies; Israel does not. Samson is released from his bondage; Israel is not from its. And in the inscrutable mystery of this polarity of achievement and failure, of action and recognition, resides the central enigma that informs and generates the tragic character whether in drama or prose fiction.

If the protagonist of the Samson tale shows us a simple folk hero sliding into the complex condition of the tragic hero, an equally clear pattern of increasing complication is found in the narrative structure of the story. At first glance, and indeed on one level, the narrative records a stripped and compressed version of the genesis, rise, and fall or decline of the epic hero. In his unusual birth, being hedged about by various taboos, and possessed of enormous and unusual strength, Samson has obvious links to the likes of Beowulf. But while the trajectory of his life is similar in its ascending and descending movement, it also betrays a more structured form than appears to the casual eye. The latter is inclined to view the incidents in Samson's career as a random succession of impulsive acts dictated by Yahweh and illustrative of the protagonist's capriciousness and violent self-gratification. And certainly this is part of the design of the story. For if Yahweh's divine intervention is to receive the maximum inscrutability necessary to the radically distant remove at which he stands from human actions and thoughts, then Samson's actions, which arise at his instigation, must be devoid of motive and discretion alike.

Nevertheless, there is another important dimension to the narrative, one which is less picaresque in character and more aesthetically structured into ordered sequences. The story breaks very neatly into sections, the first and last of which frame the others which, in turn, form a pattern of threefold repetition with variations. The central body of the tale obviously centers on Samson's adult exploits. But it is important to notice that this is focused by initial and concluding portions corresponding to a rising and falling dramatic action. The former's central event is, of course, Samson's birth, but this is preceded by the repeated triadic relation of Manoah, his wife, and the angel of Yahweh. The initial situation is one of physical barrenness, an apt personal or individual mirroring of Israel's national penchant for evil. Then there immediately appears a stunningly arbitrary but definitive counterpointing of that state with the angel's declaration: "Behold, you are barren, and have no children: but you shall conceive and bear a son" (13:3). An oblique index of Manoah's delight at this prospect is provided by his entreating Yahweh to permit a second visitation so that they may learn their parental and tribal obligations and actions. For significantly enough, Manoah and his wife are not only to

63

be blessed with offspring but with one who shall share in the national deliverance.

Granted the natural desire for extreme care in dealing with such an event, it is clear that the reader is not in need of a second angelic appearance to establish either the fact or the nature of the divine intervention. It occurs for the sake of the characters' understanding of the event, the homely and touching realism of their response, and the dramatic suspense that it creates. Only with the second appearance do Manoah and his wife comprehend that they have been confronted not with a religious man but with a divine being, who demonstrates his superhuman nature by ascending to heaven from the flame of the rock altar on which the thank offering has been made to Yahweh. The importance of this second visitation lies not in its occurence, not that the possibility of such an event is fictively established, for that has already been done. It is rather that it reveals the impact of such a happening on the characters privy to it. The physical acknowledgment of it is their prostrating themselves before the flaming ascent in the conventional gesture of obeisance before a power greater than oneself. The very conventionality of the gesture, its ritualistic quality, further defines the kind of imaginative world in which the narrative occurs: one in which the divine presence and intervention is not a unique, incredible fact to be explained away but an extraordinary and readily believable event.

At the same time, the verbal and emotional response of Manoah and his wife to the visitation demonstrates that this event is one fraught with considerable danger and arousing a kind of fatalistic anxiety: "We shall surely die, because we have seen God" (13:22). Manoah's understandable terror over the spiritual experience is allayed in the compressed but beautifully simple and commonsensical reply of his wife, which catches with profound rightness the nature of Yahweh and his people's relation to him (13:23):

> If the Lord had meant to kill us, he would not have accepted a burnt offering and a cereal offering at our hands, or shown us all these things, or now announced to us such things as these.

However inscrutable his manner and however mysterious the workings of his mind, Yahweh, we see from this comment, is neither misleadingly accepting of, nor confiding in, his worshippers. For a brief but compelling moment, these remarks of Manoah and his wife render them as fully realized human beings exhibiting concern for, and support of, each other. Then, this swiftly sketched character study is over, and the narrative sweeps forward in its rendering of the great cosmic drama of deliverance.

The next chapter inaugurates the pattern of repetition with variation that occupies the major portion of the story. From here to Judg 16:19 the narrative is structured around three major successive sequences: Samson's descent to Timnah, his journey to Gaza, and finally his entrance into the valley of Sorek. Though these sequences are uneven in length - the second is much briefer than the others - they share a number of similarities. Perhaps the most obvious and in many ways the most important is the significant role played by a woman in each one. Nor does it take us long to see that each stands in a different social and personal relationship to Samson. The first, "one of the daughters of the Philistines at Timnah" (14:2), is his wife no matter how brief and aborted their marriage; the second is the prostitute at Gaza; and the third and by far the most important is Delilah, his beloved and mistress. Clearly the three represent the major sexual relationships available to the adult male, and just as clearly each is for Samson unsatisfying and threatening to either his reputation or his life. From this, we might at first infer that a theme of what might be called romantic misogyny is being developed in which the hero's fate is designed by and his fall effected by the actions of women. Certainly something of this order lingers around the figure of Samson, particularly when the recurrent acts of betrayal are noted. Yet of itself this ignores the divine purpose operating to effect Samson's birth, the beginning of Israel's deliverance.

What happens to Samson both by way of triumph and of frustration is the result of divine intent. The former we recognize readily enough because, as in the case of the dismembering of the lion, it is make explicit that "the Spirit of the Lord came mightily upon him" (14:6). Less obvious but fully as crucial is the fact that the hero's sexual drives and frustrations stem from the same source. Chapter 13 concludes with the clipped, low-keyed declaration: "And the Spirit of the Lord began to stir him in Mahaneh-dan between Zorah and Eshtaol" (13:25). When chapter 14 opens with Samson's being immediately and unequivocally smitten by the woman in Timnah, verbalized by his terse demand "now get her for me as my wife" (14:2), the implicit causative relation surely is clear. Verse 25 is, as it were, a prelude to the three succeeding sexual encounters of the hero. In it the rationale

65

for the surge in his sexual drives is seen to be the divine spiritual disposition coordinated with his physical maturation.

The reasons for the repetition of Samson's experiencing of sexual frustration as well as other forms of thwarting reside in issues of character, theme, and narrative development. So far as the first is concerned, a number of facets of Samson's nature are revealed through the sexual motif. Initially we feel that the gruff peremptoriness of his demand of his parents "now get her for me as my wife" is only the imperious petulance of a spoiled bully who has not inquired into the true nature of his physical distinction but blandly and un-reflectively considers it a mere fact, a function of himself. But as the sexual dimension of the story develops, we are driven to recognize that at least in some measure his ostensible curtness is also a reflection of the intensity of his desire. He betrays something of the hoarse, almost strangled tone of the sexually aroused individual whose blood pounds so violently in his temples as to render him virtually inarticulate that we meet so often in the fiction of D. H. Lawrence. Samson's short statement to his father, "Get her for me, for she pleases me well" (14:3), is thus not simply or even perhaps primarily the aggressiveness of the self-indulgent. Rather it is the half-hysterical imploring of a person so obsessed that he can articulate little more than the desire itself, which threatens to consume him.

The very intensity of the passion is an index of Samson's vulnerability, of a flaw that will lead ultimately to his tragic catastrophe. At the same time, it is also a reflection of the torrential force and power existent in, and released by, Yahweh's spirit. Thus, we see that Samson's character is subsequently going to be shaped both by his emotional intensity and by his inability to bear frustration in any form. Someone not driven violently by some desire, no matter what, is not going to persist in an increasingly intense course of action of the sort requried by the divine plan for deliverance. This plan seems, among other things, to entail a calculated program of harassment, incitement, and confrontation with the enemies of the Lord until they are committed beyond a point of return. At the same time, Samson's low tolerance of frustration is also essential if there is to be a countervailing force to the dominant Philistine one; confrontation must yield to conflict and then to catastrophe for enemy and divine agent alike. In short, what at first seems arbitrary and inappropriate in the hero's character turns out to be per-fectly congruent with the theme of deliberate divine de-liverance.

Another important aspect of Samson's character which is revealed through the series of sexual encounters is his inability to profit from repeated experiences. When his wife first entreats him to reveal the answer to the riddle he has set the participants in the wedding feast, we sympathize with the reasons motivating her action, the threat of death and destruction by fire being visited upon her and her family. At the same time, we also sense the highly stylized strategy she utilizes to attain her ends, an almost stereotypical blend of rhetoric and gesture, of accusation and tears (14:16-17):

> And Samson's wife wept before him, and said, "You only hate me, you do not love me; you have put a riddle to my countrymen, and you have not told me what it is"....She wept before him the seven days that their feast lasted.

To the reader, such tactics can only appear transparent. That they do not to Samson can be attributed to two things in the main: his impercipience and his frustration at the ceremonial seven day delay in the consummation of the marriage. If to these we add a measure of masculine vanity coupled with a certain "machismo" willingness to indulge one's sexual object, we will have a fairly complete sense of what motivates his act of revealing the secret.

At the same time, Samson indicates by his initial response to his wife that it is not the logic of her argument that persuades, for he expostulates with a certain rational asperity: "Behold, I have not told my father nor my mother, and shall I tell you?" (14:16). That is, if he has not revealed the answer to the riddle to others whom he loves, why should he make an exception in his wife's case, especially since the whole point of the riddle is that the answer is a secret to be guessed. Nevertheless, he accedes, largely, we may suspect, out of weariness at and a desire for relief from her week-long crying jag. These are, in a sense, poor reasons. The fact that he acts on them indicates his unsuspicious nature and his short-sightedness and almost foolhardy willingness to endanger knowledge private to him and of the utmost importance to him. Here we get our first glimpse of the tragic hero's penchant for blindness to matters closest to him and for a kind of hubristic confidence that nothing he does or says can ever redound against him.

When one turns to the episode with Delilah, the whole situation involving the secret and efforts to learn it is greatly expanded. Instead of a singe incident, there are several. They serve to heighten dramatic suspense, to further reveal Samson's nature, particularly a kind of playful mocking and teasing rooted in his love-struck state, and to differentiate sharply between his wife's nature and that of Delilah. The brief incident with the prostitute is more of an interlude calculated to reaffirm his connection with outlaw heroes who take grave risks largely in order to demonstrate their superiority in strength, skill, and sagacity.

In carrying the gates of Gaza to Hebron, Samson is completing the second leg of his essentially triangular journey that ends back home. At the same time, the whole course inherently possesses a kind of geographical parallel to the events that is fraught with ironic implications. Samson grows up in Mahaneh-dan (13:25) midway between two towns, which suggests that if not quite a country bumpkin he at least has the simplicity, directness and lack of sophistication conventionally associated with the rustic. After the emotional and physical debacle of his wedding, he leaves his native countryside for the coastal city of Gaza where he plunges into a quite different world in an effort to obliterate his sexual frustration and humiliation through a kind of physical self-abasement.

However histrionic this may seem, it is important to remember that Samson has a measure of thematic and psychological relevance on his side, for when he returned at harvest time to claim his bride and consummate his marriage, he is refused by her father who slily pretends to have misunderstood Samson's earlier reaction to the disclosure of the riddle and so to have given her to another man. The violent rage that ensues brings death and destruction to the Philistines in a manner that escalates the conflict from border forays to lightning-like commando attacks. No mention is made here, however, of this eruption being a result of any infusion of the Lord's spirit. The only inference we can draw from the text is that Samson feels that even his relation with his wife smacks somehow of prostitution or that at least she has been rendered such in his eyes by her father's action.

From this geographical descent Samson mounts to "the top of the hill that is before Hebron" (16:3) in a manner that is both miraculous and faintly sacrificial, if, that is, we sense the similarity between carrying the wooden gates to Hebron and the dragging of the wooden cross to Calvary. Tentative though one would wish to be about this last possibility, it is clearly the case that Samson's journey is that of descent from his valley home to coastal town, and ascent to the hill of

Hebron followed by a return descent into the valley. The upward and downward movements are counterpointed in at least partially ironic fashion by those of a pasage from fertile valley to sterile sea coast to a midpoint of vantage and perspective on the hill.

Samson plunges headlong again into a romantic involvement. But here the situation is immediately a darker, more tragic one in its implications. Of the three women with whom Samson has a sexual relation, Delilah is the only one whom he is explicitly said to love. And yet immediately hard upon that revelation comes her temptation by the Philistine leaders who this time play not upon the woman's fear but her avarice. Each of them offers her eleven hundred pieces of silver if she can reveal the secret of his strength and how they can overcome it. With this we see how Samson's journey to the presumably tough coastal town of Gaza and its red-light district is an ironic foreshadowing of his discovery of Delilah in the valley near his childhood home and the town where he first saw his wife. Both the woman of Gaza and Delilah are prostitutes, but the difference is that the former is an honest one explicitly plying her trade in exchange for money and restricting her involvement to physical functions. Delilah is, as it were, a whore at heart aware of the hero's love for her and how his emotions may be manipulated to serve her greed and lust for power.

The story does not say so in so many words, but the phrase, and a highly traditional and conventional one it is, "And it came to pass afterward" (16:4 - RSV has "After this"), which bridges the Hebron vista and the valley of love, pretty clearly suggests that Samson as an individual has attained some perspective on his life and has decided that it can flourish and grow only in the fertile world of home. The overriding irony of this conclusion, of course, is that this is correct only for Samson personally. It ignores what the reader alone knows, namely, that Samson is not only an individual but also, and more importantly, an instrument of the Lord in the deliverance of Israel. Hence, Samson's love and almost immediate betrayal darken into impending tragedy for him. Strikingly enough, the rather flippant, mocking manner in which he plays with the crucial question of his secret conveys both the tragic hero's "hubris" and his ultimate conviction of his transcendent significance and worth which crystallizes in the recognition that to die is not necessarily to fail.

The elaborateness of Delilah's efforts to learn his secret are in sharp contrast to his wife's single attempt. That this is

69

an indication of the greater seriousness of the disclosure is obvious. What perhaps is not so obvious is the change in story and the change in the character and significance of the woman's interrogation. On the first occasion, Samson vehemently posed a question that captured the unassailable logic of his refusal to disclose his riddling secret. Here, however, he provides three successive answers, admittedly false ones, without a murmur. It is only when, as earlier, the issue of his love is joined that he manifests any distress (16:15-16):

> And she said to him, "How can you say, 'I love you', when your heart is not with me?"...And when she pressed him hard with her words day after day, and urged him, his soul was vexed to death.

The explanation for his shift in attitude lies in the abstract or impersonal nature of the issue and in the ritualistic character of Samson's replies. The seat of his strength and how he may be placed in bondage are issues apart from his own human individuality and character as a person; he sees his prowess now as an inexplicable consequence of his being a Nazarite, that is, someone consecrated to the deity's service rather than as an extension or authentication of his own individual nature. So far as his role as divine instrument is concerned, Samson is not enjoined to secrecy; it is only, as subsequent events demonstrate, his safety and freedom as a separate person that makes secrecy of prime importance.

The nature of his responses to Delilah's questioning shows quite clearly that it is not as an individual that he is replying. For one thing, as we have noted, there is the complete absence of objection. But even more importantly, the answers or pseudo-revelations are all couched in accordance with a pattern of magical ritual, which is nonetheless significant for being misleading. Three times he declares how he may be bound: by fresh bowstrings, by new ropes, and pinning his hair to her loom. And in two of the cases, the number seven also figures prominently, thereby accentuating the magical, folkloristic dimensions of the ritual answers. Samson can answer as freely as he does not only because his statements are false but because they do not apply to him as individual, as son of Manoah and lover of Delilah. And, in any case, so long as he comments only on how he can be bound and not on wherein his strength consists, he is immune. That Samson is playing a great and delicious joke on all concerned is clear from the celerity with which in 16:7 he glides from Delilah's double-barrelled question to a series of answers to the second part only.

70

Such a course, however, does not square with the catastrophic deliverance envisaged by Yahweh as the conclusion of the story. Were Samson to maintain his ritualized composure, an impasse would follow forcing the narrative to grind to an inconclusive stop. But Samson is not simply Yahweh's agent, he is also an individual human being, a man bitterly hurt by and incredulous at past betrayals, and a man presently deeply in love. In short, he is a man profoundly in need of someone to trust who will complete his nature and so alleviate his compulsiveness and impulsiveness alike. What he does not realize is that these last two traits are not so much his in himself as manifestations of the spirit of the Lord and so not susceptible of human alleviation. The only way they are to be purged is through tragic suffering, as Milton was to suggest in "Samson Agonistes", and through the catastrophic finale in which the tragic action is completed. Consequently, the story does not grind to a halt, but instead plunges ahead in a steadily accelerating pattern of emotional intensification.

As an individual human being, Samson cannot stand Delilah's reiterated challenge to the reality of his love. He divulges the secret that will ensure his imprisonment, blinding, and humiliation. In short, he assures his tragic fall from devastating scourge of a nation to beast of burden in a prison house. Yet this is a far cry from the theme of love's triumphant if tragic mastery of all other considerations that flickers through Shakespeare's "Antony and Cleopatra" and that Dryden rendered both simpler and more explicit when he entitled his version of the same story "All for Love: or, The World Well Lost". Delilah, though a temptress like Cleopatra, has none of the latter's nobility or final loyalty. And Samson, now that "the Lord had left him" (16:20), has none of Antony's heroic magnificence in defeat, for he has become, as he predicted several times, "like any other man" (16:17). Were Samson's story to be but one of human misfortune, frustrated desires, and shattered hopes, then it would end in the bleak vision of endless personal misery of v 21:

> And the Philistines seized him and gouged out his eyes,
> and brought him down to Gaza, and bound him with
> bronze fetters; and he ground at the mill in the prison.

The story, however, does not end here. Once again this tells us that the story is not simply Samson's personal trajectory from awesome reputation to ignoble slave, object of scorn, and figure for harmless sport. Indeed, what we find in the story's conclusion is already implicit in Samson's disclosure to Delilah. This it turns out, with deliciously appropriate irony, is not as full a disclosure as at first appears. When Samson finally can stand no more of Delilah's personal rebukes, he confides what seems to cover all the issues of source of strength and means of bondage (16:17):

> A razor has never come upon my head; for I have been a Nazarite to God from my mother's womb. If I be shaved, then my strength will leave me, and I shall become weak, and be like any other man.

True though this is, it is not quite the whole truth. Samson has been a Nazarite, at least potentially, since his pre-natal period, and apparently the vow enjoined by the angel and accepted by his parents is a lifelong one of the sort characteristic of the pre-exilic period. Yet according to the conditions imposed on the temporary vow-taker, abrogations of the vow through violation of one or another of its rules resulted in his head being shaved and then, after appropriate ceremonies were performed, "he began again to perform the period of his vow".[4] From this it would appear that a fuller version of the spiritual facts surrounding Samson's special relation to Yahweh would include the possibility of his vow's being renewed with the resumption of his abstention from the use of a razor and subject to the Lord's consent.

By now we have become accustomed to the story's narrative and thematic procedure being largely a matter of terse statement, omitted transitions, and elliptical references. Consequently, when we find the stark horror of Samson's blinding and imprisonment of v 21 being immediately followed by a laconic observation of such blithe chipperness as to appear gratuitously callous, we are alerted to its having additional implications: "But the hair of his head began to grow again after it had been shaved" (16:22). Though at this juncture there is no guarantee, there is at least the possibility that if Samson's loss of hair presaged his loss of strength, his growing of hair may anticipte the restoration of his strength. Verse 22, in other words, foreshadows that transformation of catastrophe into spiritual vindication which is the last turn of the wheel of tragedy. As a result, we are able to endure the hero's sustained humiliation in the five verses following with the clear prospect that the Philistines' unalloyed gloating is but a spiritual and moral prelude to an awful act of retribution. When, therefore, Samson finally asks the Lord directly for help, thereby at last acknowledging that he knows the true source of his strength, we sense from the intensity inherent in the words and the prayerful manner in which they are couched that no explicit answer is necessary (16:28):

> O Lord God, remember me, I pray thee, and strengthen me, I pray thee, only this once, O God, that I may be avenged upon the Philistines for one of my two eyes.

The desire of the hero and the purpose of the Lord are one: deliverance from bondage is the achievement of both and of the one through the other. In this way, the pattern of thematic action, reiterated several times through the narrative, doubles upon itself much in the manner in which the Old Testament serves as an adumbration of the New. For the chief pattern enacted in the story is that of compulsion followed by marvel which yields to betrayal and then is countered by vindication. The compulsions - sexual, agricultural, and military - all of which are forms of limitation and imprisonment, are balanced by the marvels of the dead lion, the water from the jawbone, and the carrying off of the gates. These last stand to the compulsions as the vindication of Samson and Yahweh through the destruction of the prison house stand to the betrayals by Samson's wife, the men of Judah, and Delilah. Marvels are vindications of the spiritual world even as vindications of man , and God are marvels in the natural human world. And both can exist, as the story of Samson demonstrates, only in the realm of narrative where creator and witness are one.

Chapter Five

THE CONTEST OF DARIUS' GUARDS

James L. Crenshaw

Rom time immemorial men and women have striven to discover the quality that endures the baneful effects of time's passage. A victim of the aging process themselves, they have ever sought that lasting powerful force to which they could link their own fragile lives in some meaningful way. One means of discovering what survives the vanishing aeons, and consequently of distinguishing the ephemeral from the eternal, was the question and answer dialogue. By posing a question and offering several answers with differing degrees of adequacy, it was possible to evaluate the relative merits of proposed solutions. Furthermore, the genre gave full rein to rhetorical skills, so that the seriousness of the quest was not permitted to weigh down the rhetoric. Making creative use of traditional material, rhetors developed dialogue into humorous entertainment worthy of the finest ears. Such a dialogue is that attributed to Darius' guards in 1 Esdras 3:1 - 5:3[6].[1]

The Framing Story

Like the poetic dialogue in the Book of Job, this one is also encased within a framing story, here a contest over the strongest thing in the world. Such contests are well known in comparative literature; two of them deserve special mention because of their great similarity to the one under consideration. The first, a Greek account, reports that three Samian girls told riddles while drinking at an Adonis festival, and someone put the riddle about the strongest. The first girl answered "iron", for men dig and cut everything with it and use it for every purpose. The second said "blacksmith", because he bends iron, no matter how strong, and softens it, doing whatever he pleases with it. The third proposed "penis" as strongest, since even the groaning smith is controlled by it.[2]

The other related text comes from Ethiopia, and lauds woman as strongest:

> Iron is strong, and yet fire conquers that.
> Fire is strong, and water conquers that.
> Water is strong, and the sun conquers it.
> The Sun is strong, and a storm cloud conquers it.
> A storm cloud is strong, and the earth conquers it.
> The Earth is strong, and man conquers it.
> Man is strong, and grief conquers him.
> Grief is strong, and wine conquers it.
> Wine is strong, and sleep conquers that.
> But woman is strongest of all.[3]

Such elevation of woman has produced some marvelous stories. A particularly delightful version is preserved by Adam Korczynski dating from 1698. A peasant bought shoes for his wife, and pretended to be afraid to take them home since they were not flawless. Offering them to any man who did not fear his wife, the peasant turned them over to a villager who stoutly denied that he was afraid of his wife. Having persuaded the villager to buy bread, cheese and beer for him in return for the shoes, the peasant then purchased oil and grease for the new shoes and proceeded to rub the smelly ointment all over the villager's shirt and coat, until the unfortunate villager cried out, "Stop, or my wife won't let me into her bed". Grabbing the new shoes, the peasant said, "Look, neighbors, I am fooled", and ran away, leaving the villager to pay for the food.

A Turkish version is even more humorous. A caliph of Iraq, accompanied by his vizier and jester, comes upon a man fleeing from his angry wife, and watches in utter disbelief as the man runs into a tiger's cage. While neither the caliph nor the vizier could believe that a man would prefer a tiger's roar to a wife's rage, the jester uses the occasion to get from the caliph a letter authorizing him to collect one horse from every man in the kingdom who fears his wife. The vizier, the first victim, even gives an extra horse as a bribe to prevent the jester from proclaiming far and near that the king's sage fears his wife. Some time later the jester returns, having traveled from one end of the kingdom to the other, and brings with him numerous horses and a lovely wife for the caliph.

The latter is delighted with the gift, but becomes uneasy when the jester praises the young woman loudly enough to be heard by the chief wife in the harem. Once the reason for the caliph's uneasiness is articulated, the jester requests a horse from him also. The old wife, who had overheard the conversation, supports the jester's demand, and he obtains from the exalted caliph a token that a woman rules the "sovereign" of the land.[5]

The facts of the framing story of 1 Esdras are simple, although fraught with difficulty from the viewpoint of the entire book. After hosting a sumptuous banquest, King Darius found sleep impossible. His three guards passed the night by dreaming up a contest about what is strongest, and let their imaginations run wild in anticipation of great reward for the winner. Placing their answers under the king's pillow, they awaited his summons to defend the individual responses. One wrote "wine", another, "king", and yet another identified "woman" and "truth" as strongest. Upon waking, Darius read the answers and called his lords, together with his guards whom he charged with explaining the meaning behind the enigmatic responses. The dialogue then unfolds, and the third speaker, identified as Zerubbabel, is proclaimed winner. Rather than requesting monetary reward, he reminds Darius of an earlier royal vow to return the vessels stolen from Jerusalem in 587 B.C.E. The king grants Zerubbabel's request and the story closes as it opened, with feasting and rejoicing.

Tension exists between this story and the dialogue, creating considerable irony. The framework pictures the king acting in his role as strongest; the envisioned rewards throw royal prerogative and favor into special prominence by their language and content. At the same time, the story portrays a king who falls victim to sleep, and the people themselves proclaim the winner of the contest. Within the dialogue, the king's might falters before appetite and sleep, and ultimately death conquers all over whom the verdict "adikon" (unrighteous) has been pronounced. Still, truth is hailed in regal terminology.

Implausibilities abound within the story, suggesting that it did not always belong to the larger narrative.[4] For example, the framing narrative ignores everything that has gone before, so that the two accounts cannot be reconciled. In addition, the guards themselves determine the nature of the rewards, which are supposed to be given on the basis of the written statements. Furthermore, the story seems confused about whether or not Darius was asleep.

The conclusion of the framing story has been expanded by the application of the incident to special Jewish interests. Nothing in the original framing narrative pointed to Jewish history, except for the intrusive reference to the third speaker as Zerubbabel. In this second conclusion, the sole concern is restoration of the Jerusalem temple, return of its sacred vessels, and general welfare of Jews who journey to Zion surrounded by hostile neighbors.

The absence of special Jewish interests within the original story and dialogue does not demand Greek authorship. Some evidence for translation into Greek from Aramaic does exist, particularly the use of the word "tote" (then, thereupon) for continuous narration. Praise of abstract truth stands alongside a doxology lauding the God of Truth, recalling Sirach (Ecclesiasticus) 43:1-5. Here one finds a majestic hymn about the sun that closes on a note of praise for the Lord who made it and sends the obedient sun upon its daily course. In addition, Sir 17:31-32 asks "What is brighter than the sun?" and notes that its light fails nonetheless.

The latter text lends credence to suspicion that a speech in praise of human beings as strongest has fallen out of 1 Esdras (echoes persist in 1 Esd 4:2,14,37). Sirach 17 praises humans for sovereignty over beasts and birds, and warns about unrighteousness. As tokens of divine favor, and to facilitate mastery of earth, men and women are given strength, logic, knowledge, and favor. Here we recognize a prototype of the dialogue under discussion, one that already combines the themes of endurance and ephemerality, unrighteousness, the sun's splendor, and praise of God who created one and all.

One further word seems appropriate with regard to the dialogue's provenance. Speculation about Dame Wisdom (ḥokmāh: cf. Proverbs 1-9) paved the way for praise of abstract truth, inasmuch as psalmic texts already pictured righteousness and truth as kissing one another. It follows that no reason exists for assuming Greek authorship for the dialogue in its entirety, even if it shows evidence of editorial revision.

Sapiential Traditions concerning Wine, King, and Woman

A brief look at wisdom traditions bearing upon our dialogue shows how copious were the materials from which later scribes could work. The strange workings of wine are described with pathos and humor: on the one hand, it is noted that life without wine is intolerable, while, on the other hand, it is admitted that wine can be destructive, an occasion of stumbling (Sir 31:25-31). In season wine gladdens the soul, but tests the true character of individuals. Those who fail the test posed by this gift of the vine find their strength diminished and become victims of harsh blows. Drunken fools have woe; redness of eyes are but the outer manifestations of a pathetic state in which they see strange things and utter perverse words. Neither the sting of the vine nor the resulting squalor creates in drunkards a resolve to abstinence; combined, they exert precisely the opposite effect, and victims of the cup return to the poison oblivious to blows that invariably follow (Prov 23:29-35). In truth wine is a mocker and strong drink is a brawler, leading fools astray (Prov 20:1) and bringing poverty as its hang-over (Prov 21:17). Nevertheless, since wine possesses the power to make people forget their sorry lot (Prov 31:4-7), it should be given to those who are poor and dying, and should be consumed with a happy heart, inasmuch as God has already approved it (Qoh [Ecclesiastes] 9:7). There are those, however, whose responsibility for maintaining a just society demands clarity of thought at all times. Hence wine is not for kings lest they pervert justice (Prov 31:4-7; contrast Qoh 10:17). When wine is coupled with the other great temptress, woman, even intelligent persons go astray (Sir 19:2).

Equally ambiguous are traditions dealing with the king. On the one hand, kingship is accepted as a reality with which one must reckon. Unlike prophetic and historical literature, which has an incisive critique of the concept of manarchy based on the belief that God ruled his people, wisdom literature has no clear attack on kingship as such. The wise did not, however, close their eyes to harsh reality; their proverbs recognize that old kings may become rigid and refuse to take advice (Qoh 4:13-14) and that rationality often gives way to arrogance of position when the king surrounds himself with fools (Qoh 9:17). Indeed, the proud demeanor of kings becomes the subject of mild ridicule (Prov 30:31); and sages concede that undisciplined rulers bring ruin upon their people (Sir 10:3). But the king is supreme, enjoying absolute freedom to do as he chooses (Qoh 8:2-4); consequently it is better to avoid him and his court since his displeasure signals instant execution (Sir 7:4-5). Inasmuch as God dispenses his favors through the king (Prov 21:11) and justice belongs to the royal domain (Prov 20:8), having a monarch is preferable to not having one (Qoh 5:8[9]). This ruler who searches out the unknown (Prov 25:1-7) and whose favor resembles the falling dew (Prov 19:12) is subject to the vicissitudes of history; his power may be stripped from him in a flash (Sir 11:5), and he can be corrupted (Prov 29:26). Since money speaks loudly in his ears, absolute justice comes from the Lord alone. Moreover, wisdom is stronger than ten kings (Qoh 7:19), and today's king is tomorrow's corpse (Sir 10:10). Thus kings take an inferior position to both wisdom and God.

Just as wine perverts the capacity of a king to execute justice, so too woman possesses power to destroy kings (Prov 31:3). The traditions relating to women are likewise ambiguous, as in the case of wine and the king. Many are the texts praising the wife as man's most precious "possession", worth far more than gold (Prov 31:10-31; Sir 7:19; 26:1-4, 16-18; 36:22-25). Such a treasure, the gift of God, is to be appreciated both for her ravishing beauty and sound intelligence. She is indeed the sole source of pleasure and meaning in a silent universe (Qoh 9:9), when death is preferable to life. Nevertheless, more bitter than death is the woman who cannot be trusted (Qoh 7:26), and unfortunately a man cannot entrust his soul to one woman in a thousand (Qoh 7:28). Since the wanton actively engages in bringing about man's downfall (Prov 5:3-14 and passim), and a man's wickedness is better than a woman's goodness (Sir 42:12-14), the person of discretion avoids the strange woman like a plague. Her gifts are, in fact, equally destructive; she leads her victims to the slaughter like dumb animals. Consequently one should not give himself to a woman so that she masters him (Sir 9:2); special care must be taken to shun the female entertainer whose beauty leads the best and wisest man to his doom, and to avoid dinner companions of the fairer sex who are married (Sir 9:1-9). A lack of discrimination enhances woman's seductive powers: whereas a man will choose among possible options, selecting some and rejecting others, a woman will make her well available to any thirsty traveller and open her quiver for any arrow (Sir 26:12; 36:21). The decree from of old stands over this divine gift and Satanic messenger: "you must die" (Sir 14:17). Subject to this decree, too, is the king, and the fruit of the vine passes away. Only truth is worthy of supreme sacrifice, and those who strive to the death for her soon discover that they have a powerful champion on their side - God (Sir 4:28).

On the basis of this brief resumé of traditions focusing upon wine, the king, and woman it becomes clear that the step from such material to that characterizing the dialogue under consideration is a tiny one.

Rhetorical Features within the Dialogue

Each of the three speeches makes use of a common introductory formula: "Then the first (second; third), who had spoken of the strength of wine (the king; women and truth) began and said (or began to speak)". Similarly, each is concluded with a simple word to the effect that he stopped speaking or ceased. Each spokesman makes skilful use of rhetorical questions. The first speaker sets the tone of the discussion by means of a question ("Gentlemen, how is wine the strongest?") and another to invoke assent ("Gentlemen, is not wine the strongest, since it forces men to do these things?"). The second speaker opens with a false answer in question form, only to correct it promptly ("Gentlemen, are not men strongest who rule over land and sea and all that is in them?"). Such a rhetorical question leads directly to a discussion of him who rules over them all, the supreme monarch. This speaker also appeals for favorable response ("Gentlemen, why is not the king the strongest, since he is to be obeyed in this fashion?"). But the third speech is not content with an introductory and a final rhetorical question; on the contrary, it is punctuated throughout by copious questions (1 Esd 4:14-35):

> Gentlemen, is not the king great, and are not men many, and is not wine strong? Who then is their master, or who is their lord? Is it not women?...Do you not labor and toil, and bring everything and give it to women?...And now do you not believe me? Is not the king great in his power? Do not all lands fear to touch him?...Gentlemen, why are not women strong, since they do such things?...Gentlemen, are not women strong?...Is he not great who does these things?

The third speaker boldly states his view as if only a fool would dare disagree: "Hence you must realize that women rule over you! " (4:22). Such confidence, together with the abundance of rhetorical questions throughout the speech, lead him to dispense with a final question, "Gentlemen, is not truth strongest of all?", in favor of a doxology, "Blessed be the God of truth! ".

The first two guards speak briefly and to the point; the third wanders over the broad range of ideas from earth to heavenly manifestation and further abstraction; his speech is twice as long as the other two combined. Whereas the first two spokesmen have no opportunity to respond to the opponents' arguments, but must content themselves with concise defense of their arguments that wine and the king are strongest, the third has the privilege of tearing down the opposing arguments, on the one hand, and defending his own position, on the other. In this regard, as in length, the third speaker has unfair advantage, for he can respond to both speeches.

Furthermore, the speeches display a broadening of focus at each stage in the dialogue. The first speaker sticks to the subject and shows commendable powers of logical coherence; the second introduces a new idea about man as strong, as if another speech had been devoted to that topic; and the third has two "arrows in his bow" to begin with, and even introduces such ideas as the vastness of the earth, the height of heaven and the swiftness of the sun. By modern standards the first speech is superior to the other ones, the third being more bombastic and less tightly reasoned. By reporting that the king and the nobles looked at one another (4:33), the author makes a transition within the third speech from women to truth with great ease. While concealing the slightest hint that the argument has thus far compelled assent, this observation also permits the hearers an opportunity to shift gears before a wholly different answer is defended.

The final speech sustains conscious humor at three places. The image of a man carrying in his hand his most precious possessions and dropping them to gaze open-mouthed at a beautiful woman, both funny and profound (4:18-19), witness to man's ultimate priorities. Such a discovery must have arisen from countless incidents in which man chose a living reality to lifeless things, however precious and priceless. Similarly, the observation that "many men have lost their minds because of women, and have becomes slaves because of them" (4:26), though grim (we might think of Samson, for example), must have provoked a knowing smile among those who listened with appreciation. Even the bold description of the king's love play with his favorite concubine, the otherwise unknown Apame, is calculated to evoke laughter from the king and is carried out with delicacy and apparent success (4:29-31). The reference to the king's gazing at Apame "with mouth agape" takes up the earlier theme of man's reaction to a beautiful woman, and in so doing brings the ruler down to the level of the common man. Before a woman even the king descends from his throne and becomes an ordinary supplicant, flattering and seeking special favor. Thus appropriately the

81

final verdict comes from the gathered nobles rather than from the king alone.

The strongly humorous element in the dialogue gives way before the powerful didactic note in the final discussion of truth. Here we enter the realm of morality and religion. Inasmuch as wine, the king, and woman are creatures they are subject to decay and corruption; hence the verdict for one and all is "adikon", unrighteous. On the other hand, truth has no share in unrighteousness or wickedness, and in her exists no partiality. Here justice alone triumphs, for she possesses both the power to implement justice and full knowledge of past, present and future to ensure equity. Invoked by the whole earth, and blessed by heaven, that is, God, this strongest of all things commends itself to those who are in danger of perishing. Triumphant, then, is truth. But the religious note rings forth with shattering impact, placing even this victor in proper perspective: "Blessed be the God of truth". This combination of subject matter and piety made the dialogue a favorite of Jews and Christians. The rhetoric and traditional material incorporated into the dialogue with consummate artistry set Judaism in the best light possible for Greek and Roman readers, and hence was a favorite of men like Josephus. And the religious fervor clothing the praise of truth especially appealed to Christians, many of whom, like Augustine, found therein prophecy of the Christ.

The Dialogue

The literary artistry of the dialogue is by no means limited to careful but copious use of rhetorical questions, formulae, and humor, or to didactic intentions. The arguments themselves, little masterpieces, say much in few words. We turn, therefore, to brief explication of the meaning of each component in the dialogue. We shall leave aside the intriguing question about the number of speeches in a hypothetical original, as well as the order of the speeches. Evidence does not justify certainty in these areas. The allusion to the power of wine over the king in the first speaker's argument (3:19) cannot be used as evidence for the sequence king-wine-women-truth, for the idea is central to the argument and does not address an earlier speaker's remarks at all. Nor can one remove the discussion of truth from the final speech on the basis of anything other than pure subjectivity. While such a decision may be correct, much favors retaining the discussion as the original solution to the question, "What is the strongest?". We shall examine the dialogue in its present form, even though tempted by 4:2,14,37 to suggest that a defense of man as strongest in terms of the dignity accorded him in the creation account has dropped out.

A. Wine is Strongest

The knowledge that men and women are rational creatures was not limited to ancient Greeks. While Plato's students, led by Diogenes, may have made fun of his definition of man as a thinking animal without feathers by attaching to a cock the label "philosophical man", the metaphor of human beings as rational has always seemed appropriate in discussions of their essence. "Cogito ergo sum" (I think, therefore I am) removes men and women from their environment and exalts them over all other creatures. Yet this distinctive mark succumbs to the power of the vine, whose product leads astray the keenest mind.

Besides this rational essence, an artificial distinction according to sociological status emerges early. Hence class differences surface, men and women being fitted into appropriate niches on the basis of things over which they have no control (birth) or which have nothing to do with their real selves (possessions). The latter make it possible for one person to subject others to servile obedience, for the rich can enslave those indebted to them. And, of course, there must be someone at the very top of artificial distinctions among people; this person of power and privilege acclaims himself king. Such differences pass away when wine wields its strange power, and now at long last king and lowliest subject stand equal, as do master and slave, rich and poor.

Inasmuch as women and men are thinking creatures upon whom class distinctions have been imposed, above and beyond the ordinary causes for anxiety and remorse, they are ever and again victimized by fear, pain, and sorrow. The sentence of death hangs over their heads, and fertile imagination conjures up all sorts of dangers both real and supposed. Actual pain, both their own and that of those dear to them, increases anxiety about approaching death and heightens agony caused by disappointment, intensifying to the breaking point all psychically based consternation. When wine enters the bodies of men and women, frequently the worry-prone victim of death's messengers, they forget for the moment the power of pain. In place of sorrow and financial woe come a glad heart and freedom from care, so powerful is the blood of the grape. Those who under ordinary circumstances and beset by problems of daily existence can muster minimal self esteem find limitless resources lurking within the cup, which loosens the tongue so that newfound confidence proclaims itself with complete abandon.

Rich experience has taught the values of friendship and the indispensability of fraternal loyalty; without friends or brother, one is vulnerable from every side. Consequently friendship ties and kinship bonds came to occupy a high position in the order of priorities, for nothing was too great a price to pay to assure the perpetuity of those relationships. Even a grievous offense could be overlooked lest the bond with another be severed, and great care was taken to avoid injury to a friend or brother. But persons who have their fill of wine treat such valuable relationships like ordinary refuse, and with reckless abandon pick a quarrel that leads to blows between friends and brothers.

The seasons come, and the seasons go, and with them birth and death. The strange capacity for remembering, that ability to recall selected events, thoughts, and sensations from the shadowy past, survives the powerful sway of time's monotony. Often cause for wonder and astonishment, this memory enables men and women to relive those cherished moments when time and eternity coalesced and the joyous soul cried out, "Stay, thou art so fair". Furthermore, such remembrance of sacral events opens up new possibilities for those to whom primeval event stands as both summons and demand; from its power they receive renewed redemption and ethical motivation. Still, even this astonishing memory bows in submission to the greater power of wine, and the individuals recall nothing that transpired during the drunken stupor.

Wine, then, functions as the great leveler; its mighty floodwaters sweep in the swirling maelstrom all human rationality, memory, psychic states, distinctions both real and artificial, and bonds of friendship and brotherhood. From the murky waters left by the subsiding flood one can pull their corpses, newly transformed into perverted thought, forgetfulness, joviality, boasting, camraderie, and bellicosity. "Gentlemen, is not wine the strongest, since it forces people to do these things?" Such was the brief, but truly cogent, argument of Darius' first guard.

B. The King is Strongest

The silence of the second speaker with regard to the persuasive points made by the first in defense of wine as strongest puzzles, particularly since he introduces his remarks about the king with a veiled reference to human dominance of the environment. The latter allusion is surely hyperbolic; as the divine speeches in Job 38-41 make perfectly clear, men and women never succeeded in humbling all creatures on land or sea despite the creator's command to do so (Gen 1:28). Hyperbole or not, this reference to human mastery of lesser creatures provides an excellent backdrop against which to focus the comments about ancient oriental kings. No exaggeration, however, occurs in the description of the king as lord and master. Consequently, repeated use of the word "obey" is in order (4:3,5,10,11,12); even when the word is missing, the idea of total obedience pervades the language of understatement. For example, the innocuous word "tell", which occurs frequently (4:4,7-9), carries the full weight of royal command. Whereas others must utter fruitless commands, the king need only inform his subjects of his slightest wish, and they accomplish it forthwith.

Seven times the phrase, "if he tells", occurs in the portion of the speech preserved in 4:7-9, and another time in 4:4, where it is in parallelism with "send". The sevenfold usage and the subject-matter recall Qoh 3:1-9, which juxtaposes similar human actions according to polarities. While Qoheleth arranges fourteen opposites, reduced to seven doublets, in serial fashion, our dialogue has only four opposites, three ideas being left to stand alone. In both we have the opposites kill/heal (or release), and build/cut down. Common to both, also, are references to making war (although this one falls outside the compact unit in 4:7-9), attacking, laying waste, and planting. Comparison with Qoh 3:1-9 is instructive.

For everything there is a season, and a time for every
    matter under heaven;
a time to be born and a time to die;
a time to plant, and a time to pluck up what is planted;
a time to kill, and a time to heal;
a time to break down, and a time to build up;
a time to weep, and a time to laugh;
a time to mourn, and a time to dance;
a time to cast away stones, and a time to gather stones
    together;
a time to embrace, and a time to refrain from
    embracing;
a time to seek, and a time to lose;
a time to keep, and a time to cast away;
a time to rend, and time to sew;

a time to keep silence, and a time to speak;
a time to love, and a time to hate;
a time for war, and a time for peace.
What gain has a worker from his toil?

Of these fourteen opposites only those appropriate to royal command have found a place in our dialogue. Most, however, concern emotional responses and relationships not subject even to the king's wishes. Weeping and laughter, love-making and continence, abstemious saving and reckless squandering, silence and speech, loving and despising cannot easily be brought under royal decree. The amazing similarity between the two texts suggests a common fund of traditional motifs, and perhaps, too, a tendency to place opposites over against one another in an effort to arrive at completeness.

The dialogue brings all citizens under the iron hand of the king. It mentions first those directly associated with their lord, the professional army. Subject to the king's slightest whim, the standing army moves at his command. Tossing personal welfare to the wind, and wishing only to gain favor in the eyes of the king, these courageous soldiers gladly give their lives in battle and do not consider for a moment whether the goal of the campaign justifies supreme sacrifice. With stark realism and utter simplicity the second guard describes the accomplishments of such a loyal army: they conquer mountains, walls and towers. An army spurred by royal command is deterred neither by the rugged terrain that must be traversed to arrive at the enemy's territory nor by the protective mountain upon which the fortress rests. Having been sent, the soldiers dare not return until they have trodden upon mountains, broken into walls, and levelled towers to the ground, or until their ranks are decimated so as to render further fighting utter folly. Nevertheless, even spoils of war do not belong to those who risked their lives, but are laid at the feet of him who sent them to the brink of death. Such loyalty is not limited to the army, for the subjects of the king impose upon themselves a heavy tax burden, both in produce and monies.

Twice the speaker interrupts his narrative of subjection to the king in order to point out the absurdity of such sacrifice. In the first instance he observes: "And yet he is only a man". Again the speaker notes that the king is subject to the same necessities as his subject, and thus must be vulnerable when his eyes are closed in sleep and when his mind tarries on food or drink. The speaker marvels that even when the king is utterly helpless no one lays a hand upon him or ventures to slip away to attend to personal business matters.

No better description of the king's supreme power could have been given than the following terse comment (4:7-9).

If he tells them to kill, they kill;
if he tells them to release, they release;
if he tells them to attack, they attack;
if he tells them to lay waste, they lay waste;
if he tells them to build, they build;
if he tells them to cut down, they cut down;
if he tells them to plant, they plant.

Absolute obedience despite the king's vulnerability - on this fact the second speaker rests his case.

C. Woman is Strongest, Truth Stonger Still

In the second speech the two answers, men and the king, are intimately related inasmuch as the former heightens the argument about a king's absolute power. The two answers in the third address are totally unrelated, for no logical progression moves from woman to truth. Those commentators who view the section on truth as a later addition are certainly correct in their refusal to see any necessity for it from the standpoint of logic. Since both answers stand alone, we shall discuss them in isolation. First, we turn to the defense of woman as strongest.

In a rhetorical question the speaker alludes in reverse sequence to the three answers previously put forth (king, men, and wine). Yet another rhetorical question takes up the second guard's key terms and suggests that they have been wrongly located : "Who then is their master, or who is their lord?". Denying that the king is the real lord and master, a third rhetorical question introduces the answer to be defended: "Is it not women?". The crowning argument has to do with origins; from the woman's womb came both the king and man who rules over land and sea. Moreover, those who plant the vine also were nourished by women. This is the last we shall hear of wine, save in the final summing up of the argument for truth. Evidently we must assume that the third speaker did not give much credence to the defense of wine as strongest. Precisely the reverse is the case with arguments put forth in favor of the king as strongest; the speaker takes great care to show that men face death in pursuit of a woman's favor more readily than they sacrifice themselves in obedience to the king, and to depict the power that a lovely woman wields over kings themselves. A decisive difference between the service of the king and a lover's devotion is the fact that the latter acts at his own initiative and does not wait to be commanded. Thus he toils for naught but the joy of laying everything at a woman's feet, and he faces every danger from wild beasts,[6] the darkness of the unknown, and human foes, only to bring what he gains to a woman and bask in the radiance of her smile. Furthermore, the spoil that a king's soldiers bring him ultimately adorns the gracious necks of his concubines, while the crown itself may even rest at times upon the lovely head of a woman. This is the point of the humorous anecdote - approaching burlesque - about the playful, flirtatious behaviour of the king and his favorite lover, Apame.

Twice the third speaker calls attention to a lover's powerful bond over against primary affection for parents. The strong attachment rooted in family relations counts for nought in the face of erotic allurement. Men readily turn their backs on father and mother. Another significant loyalty gives way to a woman's attraction, too. Even love of country fades when a woman enters a man's life. Forgetting parents and country, he follows a woman to foreign lands and dwells among strange people. Such seductive power inevitably eventuated in death, stumbling, sin. Source of life, woman also became an occasion of madness. Like wine, she held the power to reduce rational thought to incoherent babble.

So far the speakers have concentrated on terrestrial affairs.[7] The third speaker shifts the focus toward the skies in order to introduce one who excels over women, earth's stongest inhabitant. The sun encircles the vast earth and high heaven in a single day. Still, truth is greater than the sun. Invoked by the whole earth, and blessed by God, truth has no flaw. Wine, the king, women, and all men are unrighteous,[8] and will consequently perish. Time's relentless march tramples vineyards, topples thrones, lays women low. Above their dust, truth endures forever. To her belongs sovereignty. Before such an impartial judge and righteous ruler, proper human response is a fervent prayer that the God of truth be blessed. Concealed within the prayer, therefore, one discovers yet another answer to the question, "What is the strongest?". The masterful dialogue comes to rest in God.

Chapter Six

A MAN GIVEN OVER TO TROUBLE:
THE STORY OF KING SAUL

David M. Gunn

I am a man given over to trouble, and tossed between
two winds.
(Saul, in D. H. Lawrence's play, David)

But here is a man, all a man, wrestling with fate and
with the dark powers which hem in every man's destiny,
which limit him at every point in his effort to reach the
thing he has set before him.
(Adam C. Welch, Kings and Prophets of Israel)[1]

AS I read Welch's comment on Saul, I find myself agreeing, but asking (since Welch does not take up the point), who is fate, who are the dark powers, in this Old Testament story? The answer has to be, fate and the dark powers are one and the same: fate is Yahweh (RSV=the Lord), the God of Israel, and fate's spokesman is Samuel, the prophet of Yahweh.

Prologue (1 Samuel 8)

In chapter 8 lie the seeds of the main story. The established system of leadership by "judge" has failed. Samuel has resigned his judgeship in favour of his sons but they have turned out to be corrupt. In desperation, the elders of Israel seek a remedy in a change of system - why not have a "king" like everybody else? Why a king should be any better than a judge is of no interest to our narrator. More significant is the response of Samuel and Yahweh. Samuel is "displeased". But why? He himself has recognized his own incapacity in the matter (by abdicating on account of his old age) and it is his own sons who are the immediate cause of the problem.

89

Yahweh's reassurance - "they have not rejected you [as you suppose]" - suggests that Samuel's displeasure is on account of his own self-regard. So too Yahweh. He alone is "king" of Israel, and the people's desire for an earthly king is a personal affront.

The people, says Yahweh, have "rejected" him; and later (chapter 10), when Samuel gathers the people at Mizpah to choose a king, Yahweh's understanding of the people's request for a king as a "rejection" of his own kingship is reiterated (10:19). The term "reject" next occurs again in our story in the context of Yahweh's rejection of Saul (15:23):

> Because you have rejected the word of Yahweh he has also rejected you from being king.

The use of the motif of rejection thus formally links Saul's fate with Yahweh's understanding of his own treatment at the hands of the people. We shall return to this connection later.

Yahweh's final decision is a curt, "Hearken to their voice (obey them) and make them a king". What is the spirit of this compromise? Is it open-hearted generosity? Simple resignation? Or, bearing in mind its unwavering determination, does it conceal a deep-seated conviction that the wrongness of the people's request will inevitably become manifest, must become manifest, as if to say, "Hearken to their voice, and make them a king - and let us see what we shall see! "? Is, then, the instruction to "obey the people" an ironical one? Certainly there is little gracious acquiescence here; and Samuel's instruction to the people is equally curt.

Thus chapter 8 presents us with two figures whose potential for influencing future events is clearly great. They may also be two figures nursing a grievance. We have been warned against expecting the forthcoming experiment in kingship to be an unmitigated success.

Saul's rise (1 Samuel 9-12)

Saul's star rises brightly enough. He is fine lad who prosecutes his errand, looking for his father's asses, with vigor and a nice concern for his parent (9:5). Fate rapidly works its way into the pattern of events: the young man would have turned back but for his servant's chance find of money to provide a gift to the seer; fortuitously, also, Saul discovers Samuel at just the opportune moment. Saul's expedition, in fact, is pre-ordained by Yahweh (v 16); and Saul learns as much through Samuel's demonstration that he was expecting him (vv 23-24). Furthermore there is now a comforting hint of benevolent motivation behind Yahweh's involvement in the events - he has heard the cry of his people, we are told, and it is to be Saul who will deliver them from their enemies, the Philistines (v 16).

The story of the unlikely hero (see v 21) rapidly moves through a series of oblique disclosures to the anointing - an astonishing end to the search for Kish's asses - and to the giving of further signs as proof of the "reality" of Saul's designation as potential king ("chief", "prince" - nāgîd). The seizure of Saul by the spirit of prophecy marks him, at least momentarily, as prophet (like Samuel) and Yahweh's servant.

In all this rush of success, it is easy to miss a sentence that is destined to loom large in Saul's future. Samuel, having outlined the signs that will befall, continues:

> Now when these signs meet you, do whatever your hand finds to do, for God is with you. And you shall go down before me to Gilgal; and behold, I am coming to you to offer burnt offerings and to sacrifice peace offerings. Seven days you shall wait, until I come to you and show you what you shall do.

Nothing more is made of this instruction, though its foreshadowing in 9:13 might have given us a small clue that it is of more than ordinary significance. It sits amongst the other instructions of the prophet, a seemingly innocuous item, one amongst a number; and to lend to the feeling of the smooth flow of fortune here, the other items are quickly met and fulfilled without apparent disharmony.

The private designation of Saul as "prince" is then succeeded, in vv 17-27, by public designation as king, again the divine choice being indicated by "chance" (here the lot). Once more there is a strong negative undertone. Samuel restates Yahweh's complaint against the people who want a king. Moreover, some of the Israelites are sceptical: "'How can this man serve us?' And they despised him, and brought him no present" (10:27).

The third phase in Saul's way to the throne is the deliverance of Jabesh-Gilead. As the divine spirit had seized him and caused him to prophesy at the time of his anointing, so now it emboldens him to make a challenge to all Israel to come to the help of the besieged city. The aftermath shows us a magnanimous Saul who spares the life of those who had earlier opposed him (11:12-13; cf. David's similar response in 2 Sam 16:5-12 and 19:18-23) and who ascribes to Yahweh the victory. With this test behind him Saul's kingship is "renewed"

91

(confirmed?) "before Yahweh in Gilgal", with great rejoicing by all the people. As for Samuel's instruction of 10:8, we are left uncertain as to whether or not it has been carried out.

Chapter 12 brings us back to the grievance hinted at in the Prologue. If Saul and the men of Israel are rejoicing greatly, Samuel is not. He appears defensive, self-protective: the old has made way for the new. Is there any complaint outstanding against the old? The people respond to this sense of rejection, and bear witness loyally to Samuel's personal integrity - and thereby appear to put themselves in the wrong. If they have nothing against Samuel why then should they have demanded a king? The prophet now attacks them for their history of disloyalty to Yahweh, stressing again that since Yahweh alone is king of Israel, the demand for another king is disloyalty.

This recapitulation of chapter 8 is not insignificant. It brings home the point that the affront is still keenly felt. But we know, and the people know, that Yahweh has made a compromise and has, in fact, chosen a king. So now the terms of the compromise may be spelt out: the king must recognize his subordination to the king of kings. To hearken to the voice of Yahweh (and by implication, his prophet) and obey his commandment are absolutely essential if Yahweh is not to turn against both king and people. And to demonstrate finally that his word is indeed God's word, and that the power he represents is a power to be reckoned with, Samuel invokes the ruin of the harvest.

At no point in the the scene does anyone remonstrate with Samuel, even though it is apparent that no one is particularly convinced that the move to kingship was a wrong one (no one suggests that the decision for kingship be revoked). The people confess a sin and ask that they may not die. For most people, in the face of divine anger, that is wisdom. It is all the more significant,therefore, that Saul alone in the whole story will remonstrate directly with Yahweh or his prophet (chapter 15) and even then his self-assertion will be short-lived (and like the people here he will confess his "sin").

The scene thus ends with Samuel totally in control. He it is who will pray for the people, despite their present bad lapse, and he it is who will instruct them in what is right. "But if you do wickedly, you shall be swept away, both you and your king" (12:25). So the precariousness of Saul's position is made doubly clear as the first act of his story is rounded off. Not only is he a secondary figure in Yahweh's scheme of things, but he walks a tightrope. He is caught in the midst of a tense situation which is not of his own making and over which he has but limited control. There is likely to be little room for error in Saul's conduct as king, and if fault is to be found in him it is likely to concern "disobedience". Indeed, Saul seems a vassal to an overlord who is fundamentally hostile and thus he is potentially vulnerable as an object-lesson by Yahweh to a people who are less than totally committed to their God.

Saul the king: the Philistines (1 Samuel 13-14)

The next main section of the story opens with Saul's first major exercise of kingship - a campaign against the Philistines. Right at the beginning we get a further strong hint that success is not going to come Saul's way readily: it is Jonathan who defeats the Philistines at Geba, a point which the subsequent rumor that Saul had defeated them only serves to underline (13:4-5). In the event the Philistine army that confronts Saul at Michmash (13:5) is a massive one. Not unnaturally the people begin to desert or at least fail to rally to the king. Saul waits at Gilgal, disaster staring him in the face. He waits, the reader is told, for Samuel (v 8):

> He waited for seven days, the time appointed by Samuel; but Samuel did not come to Gilgal, and the people were scattering from him.

With this information, the tension is doubled. The Philistine threat is only one aspect of the potential disaster; with v 8 we know that here at last is the situation corresponding to the command of 10:8, and we now know (in the light of chapter 12) that it is a situation fraught with risk for Saul.

As his later explanation makes clear (vv 11-12), Saul feels it imperative to perform the proper religious rite, both to boost morale and to ensure that the Israelites are properly prepared for battle according to religious law. As earlier in the matter of Jabesh-Gilead he is decisive. He decides to wait for the tardy prophet no longer and offers the sacrifice himself. But (v 10),

> as soon as he had finished offering the burnt-offering, behold, Samuel came.

This sentence as much as any other encapsulates the predicament of Saul. He appears here starkly as the plaything of fate. Can this extraordinary timing of Samuel's arrrival be merely accidental? We cast our minds back to the sacrificial meal in chapter 9. There too all was urgency, for the prophet was "ahead of" Saul and Saul had to make haste to catch up before Samuel officiated at the sacrifice; here (chapter 13) it has been all urgency, but the urgency has been for the sacrifice to take place and it has been the prophet who has lagged behind. Saul's haste in the one scene leads to success, in the other to disaster. The remark in chapter 9 about Samuel comes back to us: "for the people will not eat till he comes, since he must bless the sacrifice".

The urgency of Samuel's attack is instructive. Brushing aside Saul's explanation of his action, Samuel declaims that Saul has disobeyed God's command (note that the propriety of the sacrifice being offered by other than a prophet or priest is not at issue) and stands condemned. Nor is the king given any opportunity to beg mercy of God. It is as though that condemnation, and the accompanying judgement, were the primary objects of Samuel's visit.

But on what grounds has Saul been condemned? Nowhere are they precisely stated, though the condemnation clearly derives from the instruction of 10:8. The answer lies in the ambiguity of the instruction: while it may seem that Saul has fulfilled the conditions of the command, in that he has waited the required seven days, the instruction also speaks of him being required to wait "until I come to you". It is the ambiguity that becomes the trap.

So Saul is caught.

The judgement also is ambiguous. At the least it means that Saul will not establish a dynasty; at the most it could mean that his kingship will come to an immediate end - for a successor is already chosen. Thus Saul will act henceforth knowing that unless he can manage to defy this destiny, he has himself no certain future as a king, while Jonathan his son has no future at all. For Saul there remains only the dignity of pressing on with the task in hand.

Jonathan's sortie against the Philistines in chapter 14 develops the motif at the beginning of chapter 13. Ironically it is Jonathan, not Saul, who exhibits military prowess; the battle also illustrates that, despite the condemnation of Saul, Yahweh is still on the side of Israel. We may be prompted to recall that amongst the more ominous tones of the beginning of the story, there was also that expression of goodwill in 9:16:

He [Saul] shall save my people from the hand of the Philistines; for I have seen the affliction of my people because their cry has come to me.

Jonathan puts his trust in Yahweh ("it may be that the Lord

94

will work for us", 14:6), wreaks astonishing havoc, and has his exploit marked at the end by a panic and earthquake that can only come from God. Not even Saul's involvement seems able to contain the extent of his victory (14:16-23).

However, no sooner has the story moved to this peak than the narrator undercuts the mood of triumph and slows down the pace (14:23-24):

> And the battle passed beyond Beth-aven. And the men of Israel were distressed that day, for Saul had laid an oath on the people.

The king imposes a fast on the army as a token of devotion to Yahweh: but this will ensnare an unsuspecting Jonathan. Precisely because of his succesful, divinely aided, initiation of the battle, Jonathan knows nothing of Saul's oath. It would seem that Saul is to be allowed a victory only at a cost - and the cost is to be exacted, ironically, through his own son, the agent of victory. The king triggers the complication by his own action, but only through the mechanism of the "chance" absence of Jonathan and the "fortuitous" abundance of honey in the forest into which the pursuit happens to move.

On being informed of his infringement, Jonathan is openly critical of his father, on pragmatic grounds: the honey has revived him ("see how my eyes have become bright", 14:29) and food would have sustained the army in a more vigorous mopping-up of the enemy. By ignoring the religious issue, Jonathan highlights the rather less pragmatic piety of the king's oath.

In fact the problem for Saul grows, for in desperation the people fall upon the live-stock of their enemies and eat it in a way that breaks the ritual law (14:31-33), so that Saul is forced to withdraw his attention from the battle and provide a make-shift arrangement in order to ensure proper cultic observance (14:34-35). In practice, therefore, the king's oath, however well intentioned, proves disastrous. It is as though God has thrown it back in Saul's face.

Worse is to come. That evening, dutifully consulting the priestly oracle before furthering the attack on the Philistines, Saul learns of Yahweh's displeasure, and when an elimination is made by lot (an ironic reminder of Saul's designation as king) it becomes apparent to the king that Jonathan is the offender. At this point the narrator presents us with another great irony, for Saul treats Jonathan, his own son, just as summarily as Samuel had earlier treated Saul when he offered sacrifice at Gilgal. No allowance is made for the circumstances of Jonathan's sin. Saul simply condemns him to death. In Saul's case, of course, there is a positive as well as a negative side to his response - negative, in that he exhibits an inappropriate rigidity of attitude; positive, in that he has done what he has done with the interests of his people at heart and at the sacrifice of his own (family) interest (as is the case with Jonathan who with simple dignity offers to die). Saul is doubly trapped, since (with unconscious irony) he has already sworn (v 39) that if it be he or his son who is culpable then he or his son should die.

So the story switches direction dramatically, moving from success to disaster; and the pious oath, which at first seems the cause of only minor complication, issues finally in a terrible dilemma for the king.

Resolution comes through the people (v 45). They too adopt the pragmatic view and refuse to allow the death of the one person who had most distinguished himself ("wrought with God") that day. Saul's dilemma is resolved, but at the cost of another oath broken (that of 14:39) and with a significant abdication of authority. In the end it is the people who rule, not Saul the king. Yet that is perhaps as it should be; for it is the ordinary, humane, commonsense view that prevails. Indeed there has been a curious shift in Saul's role in this episode. It is as though, in reaction to the circumstances of his condemnation at Gilgal, he has been playing the role of a Samuel, giving token of his acceptance of God's absolute priority over all merely human considerations (as in the oath) and demanding strict and uncompromising compliance with the divine scheme of things (as in his preparedness to execute Jonathan). It is Jonathan and the people who play the pragmatic, humane role that Saul had played at Gilgal. In a sense, therefore, in accepting the people's refusal to allow the (humanly speaking) absurd to happen, Saul becomes himself again.

Since Saul's oath really initiated the sequence of trouble, is Saul's problem to be sought within himself? Is he prone to be rash? And may we then look back to his sacrifice at Gilgal and wonder if there also he was hastily decisive, unduly pressured by events? On the other hand, the ironic, fatefully twisted circumstances of the oath, and the fortuitous, so-delicately-timed delay by Samuel at Gilgal are sufficient to bring back into focus that other perspective: Saul the victim. Whatever Saul's failings, he contends with much that lies beyond his control.

The immediate outcome of all this trouble is that no

further action is taken in the battle against the Philistines. Both sides withdraw. The section ends (14:47-52) with a brief recital of Saul's campaigns against enemies on all sides, with some measure of success; and perhaps in vv 47-48 we are indeed to see the fulfilment of Yahweh's promise in 9:16 that Saul would save the people from the hand of the Philistines. If so, the last verse of the chapter (14:52: "there was hard fighting against the Philistines all the days of Saul") may warn us that, strictly speaking, the promise leaves open the possibility of a complete reversal of fortune as well.

Saul the king: the Amalekites (1 Samuel 15)

Saul's second major exercise of kingship is his campaign against the Amalekites. The episode begins with instructions from Samuel, so that we are immediately aware that Saul is in another "obedience" situation. Samuel states his authority, implicitly reminding the king of his vassal status, and commands him to attack and destroy Amalek (the verb translated "destroy" has religious overtones and means devote to God, and so to destruction) and spare no one and nothing. Nothing is said of the earlier judgment against the king. Is Saul, after all to be given another chance?.

Saul launches his attack, but not before a characteristic gesture of magnanimity: he takes care to see that the Kenites escape. His victory is total (vv 7-8). But any surprise at the rapid and uncomplicated path to success is short-lived, for v 9 immediately establishes the pattern that has threatened from the outset: it seems that Samuel's command is broken. Saul and the people spare Agag, the king of the Amalekites, and the best of the livestock. Yahweh sees here defiance and "repents" of having chosen Saul. Accordingly, next morning, Samuel arrives, angry, in Gilgal to meet Saul.

There is subtlety in the writing here. At first all looks black for Saul. Samuel is told of Saul that "he came to Carmel, and behold, he set up a monument to himself". Then on meeting Samuel at Gilgal Saul greets him with "Blessed be you to the Lord; I have performed the commandment of the Lord" (15:13). It looks as though a self-regarding Saul is now trying to deceive the prophet. But then, a shift. To Samuel's demand, "What then is this bleating of the sheep in my ears?", Saul replies, apparently without embarassment, that the noise issues from the best of the Amalekite livestock which has been brought here - to sacrifice to Yahweh. Now we have a completely different view of what is going on: to be sure, Saul and the people had not "devoted to destruction" the best of the livestock on the spot, at the city of the Amalekites, but that was because they had decided it would be more appropriate to devote it to Yahweh at the god's own sanctuary.

The only point in his speech that may make us question his sincerity is that he speaks of "the people" as having spared the animals and not of himself. Yet this need not be an indication that Saul is trying to side-step responsibility, and so knows at this stage that he has done something seriously wrong. A more sensitive reading of v 9 might recognize a complexity of rhetorical style: "Saul and the people spared Agag and the livestock" may be read as "Saul spared Agag, and the people spared the livestock", or, as we would say in prosaic English, "Saul and the people spared Agag and the livestock, respectively). Read thus, vv 8-9 and 20-21 match closely. No, Saul is clearly unaware of significant wrong-doing.

Characteristically, Samuel wishes to hear nothing more and sets out his accusation. But again Saul replies, unabashed, amplifying his earlier response (15:20-21):

> I have obeyed the voice of the Lord: I have gone on the mission on which the Lord sent me, I have brought Agag the king of Amalek, and I have devoted to destruction (RSV=utterly destroyed) the Amalekites; and (RSV=but) the people took of the spoil, sheep and oxen, the best of the things devoted to destruction, to sacrifice to the Lord your God in Gilgal.

This is a splendid reply, right down to the note of irritation breaking through at the end in Saul's designation of Yahweh as "your God". The reply is unanswerable - or nearly so. This time God has jumped to conclusions. When the best of the livestock has been sacrificed, the devotion to destruction of all Amalek will be complete. The people had wished to pay special honor to Yahweh while fulfilling the spirit of his commandment.

The explanation is unproveable, but surely plausible. There is only one question mark: what were Saul's intentions for Agag, whose life was spared? We are not to know. Probably he, too, was to be slain in Gilgal, in honor of the god. Still, a tantalizing doubt remains (Agag himself seems to have been hopeful of a better fate). Perhaps the magnanimous Saul really had made a decision to flout Yahweh's commandment! Yet, significantly, Samuel does not challenge the king on that point. He chooses to ignore the explanation altogether and to respond merely with rhetoric (v 22). The real point of the scene is that Saul is long since doomed so that any justification for his condemnation is irrelevant. As with the command to wait at Gilgal, the command to destroy Amalek may be interpreted in such a way that Saul be deemed to have disobeyed it. The privilege of interpretation belongs to God. Saul, therefore, whatever his precise intentions, is bound to be convicted on a technicality.

The king now realizes that he is trapped once again and that he can do nothing other than submit. Like the people in chapter 12 he confesses that after all he has sinned (recognizing that he cannot contest Yahweh's - or his prophet's - definition of "sin") ; and only now as he plays the penitent, does he use the initiative of the people as an excuse. So he asks pardon and requests permission to be allowed continued access to the worship of God. The reader knows now, however, that this gesture is useless. Samuel rejects Saul as king, on Yahweh's behalf, and turns the robe-tearing to his purpose of judgement: the kingdom is torn from Saul "this day" and given to a neighbor who is "better" than he. Thus the judgement of chapter 13 is confirmed. But while the phrase "this day" conveys immediacy, and the term "neighbor" suggests specificity, the judgement still is as ambiguous as the first rejection uttered at Gilgal. All Saul can truly know is that he finds no favor with God; the moment of his removal from the throne is still not disclosed to him. Nor, Samuel adds, will Yahweh repent of his action (v 29).

The rest of the scene is one of pathos. Saul asks for at least a token show of honor before his people, and Samuel, with little to lose - after all, he knows now that Saul is irretrievably doomed and that Yahweh, in due course, will be vindicated - accomodates him. So, ironically, the scene ends with the "disobedient" Saul worshipping Yahweh.

Embedded amongst the last few lines of the episode (lines which function also as the first of the next episode) is the summary sentence (v 35): "So the Lord repented that he had made Saul king over Israel". It is as if to say that the episode has been about not only Saul's sin but even more, perhaps, Yahweh's "repentance" (a term which, in the context, clearly has connotations of change of heart/attitude). The sentence, of course, picks up the theme of v 11 (Yahweh to Samuel: "I repent that I made Saul king...") ; and the remarkable contradiction in v 29 (Samuel to Saul: "And also the Glory of Israel will not lie or repent; for he is not a man, that he should repent"). What does Samuel really believe? Does God "repent" or not? The discrepancy focuses our attention on the nature of God's "repentance" and raises questions about it.

On the one hand, the word of Yahweh to Samuel in verse 11 sounds straightforward enough. Because Saul has broken his commandments (as Yahweh sees it), Yahweh has repented of giving him the kingship; that is, he will now take the kingship away. On the other hand, indicators in the story so far (including chapter 15) have suggested that the basis of the judgement against Saul, the "repentance" of Yahweh, is more complex than this simple explanation ("because") suggests. Yahweh's dealings with Saul are, shall we say, less than impartial. There seems to be more to Yahweh's "repentance" than v 11 discloses. The effect of vv 11, 29 and 35 (taken in concert) is to reinforce that feeling.

Saul's rejection as king by Yahweh is beyond all further doubt. The remainder of the story is a matter of either how the rejection will be implemented in practice, or whether Saul can cheat his fate. Despite, or, perhaps, because of, foreknowledge of his fate as decreed by God, Saul will strive almost to the last to maintain his hold on the kingship. To this extent he will retain a spark of independence as a character over against divine intentions. Yet paradoxically the more he is to struggle against his fate - which from now on is increasingly embodied in the figure of David - the more he himself becomes fate's agent. In this regard, as in others, the reader will find some interesting parallels between this story and that, say, of Sophocles' "King Oedipus" or Shakespeare's "Macbeth".

Saul and his rival: David at court (1 Sam 16-19:17)

The new phase in the story introduces David and explores his relationship with Saul at court. From the outset it is clear to the reader that David is to be Saul's successor, but Saul is left to divine that for himself. The anointing of David is carried out by subterfuge involving, ironically, the pretence that the real purpose of Samuel's excursion is to offer a sacrifice. Like Saul, David is a "least likely hero", the youngest of the brothers. Like Saul, too, he is a handsome youth. One wonders whether it is with conscious or unconscious irony that the narrator, having had Yahweh deliver his fine sentiments in v 7 ("Do not look on his [Eliab's] appearance....Man looks on the outward appearance but Yahweh looks on the heart"), introduces David with no other recommendation than that David "was ruddy, and had beautiful eyes, and was handsome". Presumably, however, the outward appearance is fortuitous (or perhaps a concession to man's weakness!); we have already been told that Yahweh's choice was of "a man after his own heart" (13:14). If, looking back to Saul's anointing, we wait for God's "command" to David, we wait in vain. Where Saul's kingship had been immediately hedged around with provisions, David's is left open. No trap is set for the new king. Clearly David's fate has been marked out very differently from Saul's.

As earlier with Saul, the spirit of Yahweh comes mightily on David. Yahweh is with him. For Saul, on the other hand, the experience is reversed (16:14):

Now the spirit of the Lord departed from Saul, and an evil spirit from the Lord tormented him.

Here for the first time explicitly we have Welch's "dark powers". Again we confront the theme of Saul the victim and this theme extracts our sympathy during our growing alienation from the ever more moody, jealous and violent Saul.

There is no flabbiness in the narrative at this point. By the cruellest of fate's tricks, no sooner is David anointed and Saul unwell (poisoned by Yahweh, one might say) than his own servants are recommending David as the cure for his sickness. The economy of plot is superb and the irony of the situation that is created is quite overwhelming. In many respects 16:14-23 is the rest of the story in microcosm. With an introductory nudge by fate, Saul delivers himself into the hands of David. The king provides the youth with the opportunity to gain the status of an alternative king, and Saul becomes totally dependent on David's goodwill for his survival. Thus, right at the beginning of his career, David is shown to have the upper hand - as befits God's new servant.

Just as Saul's rise to prominence had been pictured in several stages, so now with David. Secretly anointed, then brought to court in a role ancillary to the king, he is finally put to public test. Saul's achievement had been to rally his fellow Israelites and, as a conventional soldier, to lead them successfully in battle at Jabesh-Gilead. David's achievement is to overcome, singlehanded and unconventionally, the champion of the Philistines and with him the whole army. Thus again David is marked out as enjoying the favor of providence in a most remarkable way. Moreover, the narrator goes to some pains to show that David proves himself in the face of Saul's impotence (and that of everyone else) and quite deliberately without aid from the king (17:38-39.).

However, more than David's opportunity and success as soldier and courtier is significant for his advancement. There is an emotional web spun around him in which Saul becomes enmeshed. In 16:21 we learn that Saul came to love David greatly. Likewise, no sooner has David won his victory over Goliath than we are told (18:1): "The soul of Jonathan was knit to the soul of David, and Jonathan loved him as his own soul". Saul's sudden eruption of jealousy at the public acclaim of David, and his realization that David poses a menace (18:8), is thus vastly complicated. The struggle with David is henceforth conducted in the context of a love-hate relationship, and the story, inasmuch as it may be considered a mirror of the human condition, gains in intensity and sophistication.[2]

From this point on Saul becomes locked (unknowingly?) in a contest with the will of fate, represented by the "man after the Lord's own heart", David, and from this point on the negative side of his character comes increasingly into view. Humphreys (1978) rightly speaks of the "disintegration" of Saul, though I think the disintegration is not total.

Given God's incitement of Saul to jealousy and madness, of Saul's increasing entanglement with David, and of Saul's inability to damage David's interests, every move Saul makes against David only enhances his rival's prospects. He makes him captain in order to get him out of court (18:12-6) but with the result that David is yet more successful, so that "all Israel and Judah loved David" (18:16). He tries to kill him by proxy, using the Philistines as agents and his daughters as bait (we are reminded of David's proxy killing of Uriah, in 2 Samuel 11). The first first attempt ends in failure - David, like the folktale hero, succeeds in his impossible task - and Saul is put in the wrong by having to break his promise. The second attempt also fails and he is forced to give David his daughter. He is thus even more enmeshed with David: indebted to him for his harp-playing/healing and his military service, and tied to him through Jonathan's love and his daughter's marriage.

When Jonathan achieves reconciliation between Saul and David the avenging spirit of Yahweh intervenes destructively (19:9-10). So David escapes from court aided by Saul's daughter, no less (19:11-17).

Saul and his rival: David at large (1 Sam 19:18-23:29)

The next stage in the story begins with Samuel openly

engaged in helping the king's enemy. The spirit of prophecy, which had earlier marked out Saul's election (10:10-12), is used now to circumvent his purpose (19:19-24). Saul is reduced to impotence before Samuel by being thrown into an ecstatic frenzy. Thus the spirit of prophecy functions like the spirit of evil. Both are weapons in the hand of God.

Again Saul cannot win. As the story progresses, Jonathan, who has acted as a mediator between Saul and David, tends to identify with David more and more (Jobling speaks of a "self-emptying"). While we may admire Jonathan's loyal commitment to his friend, the concomitant of that love is a curious naïveté as regards his own father's position. Failing to see that David represents any threat to his father, Jonathan is reluctant to acknowledge that Saul actually intends David harm (20:1-7) - hence the facility with which he is prepared to aid his friend and, as the reader may see it, betray his father.

At the heart of his naïveté is a simplistic view of good and evil, seen typically in the following comment (20:13):

> "Should it please my father to do you harm, Yahweh do
> so to Jonathan and more also, if I do not disclose it to
> you and send you away. May Yahweh be with you, as he
> has been with my father".

That Saul's attempt to harm David might be a direct result of Yahweh's intervention, Yahweh's having been "with him", or that good and evil might both belong in the repertoire of God, seems to be beyond Jonathan's understanding. The rest of his speech is full of awful irony, right down to the final invocation (v 16): "And may the Lord take vengeance on David's enemies". Saul's isolation here is doubly underscored.

Even in the face of Saul's fiercest anger (20:30-34) Jonathan cannot comprehend the king's predicament. And again it is an irony typical of Saul's fate that when, in an upsurge of mad anger, he casts his spear at his own son, as he had done in the past at David his rival, his action only drives Jonathan closer to David (as Jobling nicely observes).

With chapter 21 we follow the fortunes of the fleeing David. First he approaches the priests at Nob and, taking a pragmatic view of his ritual obligations, persuades (deceives?) Ahimelech the priest to give him provisions in defiance of religious law. Then, with Goliath's sword in hand, he flees - to the Philistines! David certainly has panache. The story is not without its point for Saul. We see once again the contrast between Saul and David. Saul the pragmatist is condemned by Yahweh (chapter 13, and compare the ironic reversals of chapter 14). David the pragmatist finds only favor. And from this scene leads a thread to yet another failure on Saul's part to David's advantage. In chapter 22 the king of Israel who delivered Jabesh-Gilead and protected the Kenites, now has his own priests slaughtered. Once again there is heavy irony in the writing, as we can see if, as we read the climax of the scene (22:18-20) we also remember the circumstances of Saul's condemnation in chapter 15 (v 3):

And Samuel said to Saul: "...Now go and smite Amalek, and devote to destruction (RSV=utterly destroy) all that they have; do not spare them, but kill both men and women, infant and suckling, ox and sheep, camel and ass".

And Nob, the city of the priests, he put to the sword; both men and women, infant and suckling, ox and ass and sheep, he put to the sword.

And whereas Agag was spared in the one episode to Saul's eventual discomfort, Abiathar now escapes to David's considerable advantage (cf. 23:6); for with the magical "ephod" David has the possibility of direct access to information belonging to the divine world of foreknowledge, so that no amount of double dealing (the treachery of Keilah, 23:8-13, or of Ziph, 23:19-24) can do him harm.

The contrast with the earlier Saul is furthered with David's triumph at Keilah, rescuing the city from the oppression of the Philistines, echoing Saul's deliverance of Jabesh-Gilead from the oppression of the Ammonites, while the extent of Saul's continuing disintegration is brought sharply into focus with Jonathan's further movement towards David's position (23:16-18):

"Fear not! For the hand of Saul my father shall not find you; you shall be king over Israel, and I shall be next to you: Saul my father also knows this." And the two of them made a covenant before the Lord.

Though there is still naïveté here ("and I shall be next to you"), the covenant with David is made with an awareness, at least, of the real challenge to Saul that David represents. The last clause of the speech is also significant: it gives us a strong hint that Saul is near the end of his tether, ready to capitulate. With his conscious espousal of David's cause, Jonathan ceases to have any distinct function in the story (Jobling).

Saul and his rival: Failure (1 Sam 24-27:4)

The story now enters a new stage of development: the roles of pursuer and pursued are reversed. Two episodes with Saul falling into David's hand (chapters 24 and 26) frame a picture of David as an aggressively successful outlaw captain, winning booty and wives and making inroads of power into Judah itself (chapter 25). And fate, which has played against Saul at every turn, now plays for David even to the convenience of Nabal's sudden death ("The Lord smote Nabal", 25:38), and all with a minimum of bloodshed or violence (contrast Saul at Nob, chapter 22).

David's restraint is remarkable when he has Saul in his power: "The Lord forbid that I should do this to my lord, the Lord's anointed" (24:6; cf. 26:9). While Saul pits himself against Yahweh's decree, David rests confident in the providential care of God, allowing the final initiative against Saul to come from elsewhere. Yet while David's restraint provokes our admiration, it is admiration tempered by the knowledge that the restraint is exercised in the most favorable of conditions, despite surface appearances to the contrary (the outlaw life). David can afford restraint, Saul cannot.

Indeed, nestling between the two accounts of "restraint", chapter 25 nicely pictures another, less presentable, side to David. Precipitously he intends violence against a defenceless man who had refused to pay out for "protection" (note the repetition of "sword", and the four hundred men, in v 13), and he is only just saved from "bloodguilt" (vv 26, 31) by the fortunate intervention of the persuasive Abigail.

The incidents of chapters 24 and 26 appear to destroy what remains of Saul's spirit of independence. The scene in the cave of En-gedi (24:8-22) ends with Saul speaking of "my son David" and "I know that you shall surely be king"; that at Hachilah (26:17-25; notice again the hand of Yahweh in the action, 26:12) leads to a recantation by Saul and self-abasement: "I have done wrong; return, my son David...Behold, I have played the fool and erred exceedingly" (26:21). In the event David throws back Saul's gesture of reconciliation in his face and flees to the Philistines at Gath; and, for his part, Saul, having blessed his rival (v 25), gives up the pursuit (27:4). We are now ready for the last phase of the story - Saul's removal from the kingship and his death. The latter has been neatly foreshadowed in David's response to Abishai (26:10):

As the Lord lives, the Lord will smite him; or his day shall come to die; or he shall go down into battle and perish.

Saul's end (1 Sam 27:5-31:7)

The scene opens on David among the Philistines, playing a double game and serving his own, and Israel's, ends. As Saul had done, so now he campaigns against Israel's traditional foes - "the Geshurites, the Girzites, and the Amalekites" (27:8). Unlike Saul (with the Kenites and King Agag) David spares no one; like Saul he brings back (but to the Philistines, not to Yahweh at Gilgal) the best of the booty - with impunity.

The speculation about Saul's death in 26:10 and his capitulation in 27:4 lend ominous overtones to 28:1, where we are told that "the Philistines gathered their forces for war, to fight against Israel". The central episode of the section is Saul's consultation with Samuel. The episode begins (28:3) with brief mention of Samuel's death and burial, together with a yet to be explained note about Saul having put the mediums and wizards out of the land (an act of piety). The Philistines have confronted Saul and Israel at Shunem/Gilboa. Saul is dismayed. The wording of this introduction (28:4-5) is notable, for it is strongly reminiscent of two other fateful confrontations between Saul and the Philistines, the first at Michmash/Gilgal (13:5-7) and the second at Socoh/Elah (17:1-2, 11).

When Saul seeks guidance from Yahweh, he is met with silence (cf. 14:36-37). Once again his subsequent behavior is triggered by the action (or, as here, the inaction) of God. As though re-living that day at Gilgal, he takes matters into his own hands. He does what he himself has decreed is unlawful (or so the story implies) and seeks a medium. With subtlety, the narrator conveys nuances of tension, suspicion and fear among king, medium and prophet, who is still very much alive in death. That Saul should even at this stage seek out the advice of his long-standing antagonist, who has decreed his fate in terms both decisive and yet ambiguous, invokes pathos. Having struggled with that foreknowledge, Saul now seems unable to bear further ambiguity. He needs certainty (we might usefully compare Macbeth) and is paralyzed without it. So he is prepared to humiliate himself again before the prophet.

Typically, Samuel's response to Saul (v 16) is uncompromising. But this time, for the first time, there is no ambiguity. Saul is a dead man; his sons, too, are to die (and so there can be no question of their succession); and the people (the word translated "army" in the RSV also means "people") will be delivered into the hands of their enemy (28:16-19; here the threat of chapter 12 comes to fulfilment). And at last the time is fixed - "tomorrow". The implication for Saul is that his life's achievement is to be blotted out. Israel is to revert to where it was at Saul's first appearance, blighted by foreign conquest.

The scene comes to a climax in Saul's collapse in fear (v 20). No heroics here, but another tone, of resignation. Saul is weak from fasting (again the dutiful act of piety before battle, reminding us instantly of that earlier engagement with the Philistines, in chapter 14, and the story of the oath). His fear is real enough, but the narrator restores his dignity by shifting the focus from the weakness occasioned by fear to that occasioned by actual lack of food. The woman's rather motherly concern and the sudden intrusion of mundane incidentals - Saul sitting upon the bed, the kneading of the bread - serve the same purpose . We are moved with Saul from the high world of destiny to the ordinary world of subsistence. Saul eats and accepts life, for food is the most elementary concomitant of life. Jonathan had broken the fast unwittingly and found himself condemned by his highly "principled" father for infringing the divine law. Deliberately now Saul breaks the fast and signals for the last time a willingness to sit loose from the constrictions of the sacral world. He again becomes Saul the pragmatist, the Saul who was brought to recognize the futility of a sacrifice of Jonathan in the interests of a rigid piety.

In the light of Samuel's words Saul's action can be little more than a token gesture. Yet it is typical of him that in the end he faces life, even when he knows that this time life holds in store only death. Without further word he eats and goes back into the night.

Immediately the narrator turns back to David, who is enjoying his remarkable fortune in being released from involvement in the forthcoming battle against his own countrymen - released, moreover, with blessings coupled with assiduous advice. Then, almost as rapidly as it had arrived, the good fortune is replaced by ill: Amalekites have raided David's base at Ziklag and carried off his people. Even in this calamity, however, there is good fortune almost beyond belief. In sharp contrast to David's own practice against them, the Amalekites have killed no one, but simply carried off all, wives and children, alive. Fate lends a further hand in the "chance" encounter with a former Amalekite slave who can guide David to his goal. David, like Saul before him (chapter 15), wins a swift victory. The spoil is the Amalekites' undoing (as it was Saul's undoing), for they are "scattered abroad", celebrating their successful raid and the great booty they have taken. Thus David takes them unawares. He spares none within his reach. Furthermore he rescues everyone and everything that belongs to him (30:18-19).

Behind this contrast of David's good fortune with Saul's obstacle-strewn path, lies the seemingly arbitrary disparity in God's treatment of these two men. As David carries off the spoil ("This is David's spoil", say the people as they drive off the livestock), lays down rules for its division among his own men ("it is what the Lord has given us", he says) and makes presents of it to his friends, Saul faces the Philistines and death at Gilboa. Samuel's words of rejection still ring in our ears (15:19, 28:17):

"Why did you not obey the voice of the Lord? Why did you swoop on the spoil and do what was evil in the sight of the Lord?"

"Because you did not obey the voice of the Lord and carry out his fierce wrath against Amalek, the Lord has done this thing to you this day".

The thematic statement is plain. Good and evil come from God. He makes smooth the path of some; the path of others he strews with obstacles. He has his favorites; he has his victims. The reasons, if reasons exist, lie hidden in the obscurity of God's own being.

Saul's death (chapter 31) is recounted in a simple, matter-of-fact, style. Perhaps the true climax of the story has already come, in chapter 28, with the last confrontation of Saul with Samuel. Within a few sentences we learn of the death of the sons (as prophesied). There is a moment of tension as Saul's last request to be allowed at least a dignified death is refused. But the pragmatic Saul acts typically. For the last time he takes matters into his own hands (quite literally now) and kills himself. It is a fine ending, in the best "Roman" fashion.

Epilogue (1 Sam 31:8 - 2 Sam 2:7)

As Samuel had predicted, the battle is a disaster for Israel;

the focus, however, is still upon Saul. If dignity has marked the manner of Saul's death, humiliation is still its aftermath: the Philistines hew apart the corpse (so now he is like Agag) and pin the body to the walls of Beth-Shan. Dignity, however, is quickly restored: the inhabitants of Jabesh-Gilead, in an action of striking loyalty to the man who had delivered them from the Ammonites so long ago, see to it by rescuing and burying the body, that he suffers no further humiliation. David now stands ready to receive the gift that has long since been his. Dramatically he dissociates himself from Saul's death and underscores his own previous restraint (2 Sam 1:1-15), and movingly he grieves for the dead (1:17-27). There is emotional resolution in the epilogue, particularly through the poem of lament, so that we are prepared finally for the decisive action of the closing segment. David consults Yahweh, goes up with his consent to Hebron and is anointed king over Judah. Samuel's prophecy has come as close to fulfilment as matters for the story. The rest of the country (the north) will come inevitably to David, as is clear from the tone of authority and firm resolve of the final speech (in which, cleverly, the theme of Jabesh-Gilead - representing now the north - is neatly merged; 2:5-7):

> So David sent messengers to the men of Jabesh- Gilead and said to them, "May you be blessed by the Lord, because you showed this loyalty to Saul your lord, and buried him. Now may the Lord show steadfast love and faithfulness to you! And I will do good to you because you have done this thing. Now, therefore, let your hands be strong and be valiant. For Saul you lord is dead, and the house of Judah has anointed me king over them".

Concluding observations

This story is about kings and kingship: the people want a king, their god grants them their wish and chooses one (the name Saul means something like "asked for"); the king, however, is subsequently rejected by the god and, after a struggle, a new king acceptable to him is established. In the process the attitude of the god to the institution of kingship appears to have moved from, at the outset, open hostility or at least reluctant acquiescence, to, at the close, acceptance and a commitment which is seen at its best in the god's wholehearted identification with the cause of the new king, David.

Saul appears to be a victim of this transition. From the moment of his anointing the future is loaded against him (the instruction of 10:8) and from his establishment as king in chapter 11 fate becomes his active antagonist, thwarting and twisting his every move. His rejection seems calculated and contrived. Yet the demands made upon Saul and the obstacles placed in his path are conspicuous by their absence from David's experience. David is given a free hand and can do no wrong in the eyes of God, even where he acts as Saul has acted before him. David is a favorite, Saul a victim. Why?

As we have already seen, the story hints at an answer. Early in the story Yahweh is depicted as a jealous god. He resents the people's cry for a king, which he interprets in terms of disloyalty to himself. Yet the status quo is clearly unsatisfactory. Saul, therefore, is kingship's scapegoat. Yahweh responds to the people's cry, but through Saul he "demonstrates" the weakness of human kingship (about which he has warned): through Saul's "disobedience" the people, temporarily delivered, are once again reduced to enslavement. Thus God's initial hostility is vindicated and the way is open for him, freely now and out of his own gracious benevolence, to bestow kingship anew and on new terms (with a David, not a Saul, as king). Ironically, the emergence of David as a candidate for kingship is in no small way due to Yahweh's activation of Saul's jealousy. The story, therefore, is also a story about Yahweh's "repentance", about a god's change of mind and its repercussions upon humanity.

But the narrative raises further questions. Is Yahweh's resentment reasonable? Is his subsequent treatment of the two figures morally explicable? Such questions are raised in various ways. At the level of plot, characters are confronted with decisions which involve assessing the relative importance of religious demands and duties over demands and duties of other kinds (such as of friendship, family, kingship); the judgements against Saul, startling in their severity, conspicuously ignore his explanations and the evidence of his "good faith". If he is culpable in breaking Yahweh's commandments it is surely more technical than moral culpability. At the level of the reader's overview, questions about the ultimate basis of God's actions are raised by suggesting that jealousy and a shaken self-esteem may play key roles, and by the striking disparity of treatment between Saul and David. If we are to condemn Saul for his jealous persecution of David, how much more is Yahweh to be condemned for his jealous persecution of Saul? That good and evil appear to be equally at God's disposal is also a provoking datum. Fate, it would seem, can be kind or it can be cruel, but mankind must not imagine that it can account for that kindness or cruelty in any given instance by appeal to some transparent rational or moral order. There is clouding emotion and unreason in God as there is in man. Yahweh can pour out his grace upon Israel, upon David, and even upon Saul; but Yahweh has also his dark side.

Samuel is God's spokesman and agent. He is, like his master, jealous of his own status, for he represents an awesome power; he is, like Yahweh, sometimes quick to anger and impatient of the complexities of human action and motivation. For him the will of God is the only reality: the decree of God is therefore absolute and unchallengeable. He is thus regarded by other mortals as a dangerous man (16:4), for in him one comes perilously close to God himself. David, the favored of God, finds himself moving with the tide of fortune and so is able freely to engage with the divine sphere and take action which would be death to another. For their part, the people tread warily, pay their respects to God, and bend when they sense they must bend.

What of Saul? He is not Yahweh's enemy through his own choosing. His role as king is thrust upon him by God. He constantly ascribes what success he enjoys to Yahweh. He is attentive (to the end) to the ritual acknowledgement of Yahweh. Indeed both times he is found guilty of breaking Yahweh's commandment he has done what he has done in order to offer sacrifice to Yahweh. He is prepared to acknowledge his error (whether comprehendingly or not), submit to God and, even in rejection, worship him. Saul is not disloyal to Yahweh.

In the light of this discussion it is reasonable to argue that although he does exhibit character "flaws" - he can be accused of being, at various times, rash, jealous and violent - Saul's downfall cannot be ascribed to these factors alone. First he is a victim of fate, and only secondly is he his own enemy. Whatever his faults - and some of these are bequeathed, or at least encouraged, by God - it is his fate, dictated by Yahweh, that eventually whatever he puts his hand to should be turned against him.

He is not pictured as a great hero. He takes a splendid initiative (but again at Yahweh's instigation) in summoning Israel to Jabesh-Gilead, but then, as elsewhere, there is little or no focus on his capacity as a warrior. His courage is undoubted, but it emerges in his capacity as a leader prepared to rally against an enemy, not in the personal combat which distinguishes a Samson or Achilles (or a David or Jonathan). Yet he does have courage and he has great fortitude, which we see to advantage in the story of his dogged struggle to maintain his throne and his kingdom, from chapter 16 onwards, as well as in the way he faces death at the end. He can be generous and magnanimous. Apart from the small band of disaffected who gather about David, there is never any suggestion in the story that the people as a whole wish to reject him. He commands extensive loyalty - a motif that surfaces significantly at the end of the story (the men of Jabesh-Gilead).

Set against Samuel he is positive - all life; set against David he is negative - gloomy, suspicious, doom-laden. As is true of the story of King David in 2 Samuel, the narrative discloses a central character of complexity, painted in tones that are either carefully muted, or (if some of the individual tones are strident) that give an impression of subtle modulation.

But if one asks why, in the last analysis, Saul engenders sympathy and demands to be considered a tragic figure, the answer lies less in the matter of personality than in his fundamental predicament - Saul the victim of God, the man who struggles against the perversity of fate. It is by virtue of his predicament that, despite all his faults (and a tradition of interpretation which, for dogmatic reasons, has been obliged to find against him), he has remained a figure of attraction to countless readers. For that struggle, for many men, is their own lot.

NOTES
INDEXES

NOTES

NOTES TO PREFACE

1   Norman Petersen [Literary Criticism for New Testament Critics (Philadelphia: Fortress, 1978)] holds the historical and literary methods together, even as a classic handbook by René Wellek and Austin Warren [Theory of Literature (New York: Harcourt, Brace and World, 1956)] gave important place to both.

2   The Enjoyment of Literature (New York: Simon Schuster, 1938), quoted from Mary Esson Reid, The Bible Read as Literature (Cleveland: Howard Allen, 1959) 191.

3   Reynolds Price, A Palpable God (New York: Atheneum, 1978) 12-14.

4   The number and complexity of discussions relative to Biblical studies have grown enormously in recent years. See the experimental journal, Semeia. Also David Robertson, The Old Testament and the Literary Critic (Philadelphia: Fortress, 1977); Norman Petersen, Literary Criticism (see above, note 1); Daniel Patte, What is Structual Exegesis? (Philadelphia: Fortress, 1976); Robert Detweiler, Story, Sign and Self: Phenomenology and Structuralism as Literary-Critical Methods (Philadelphia: Fortress Press; Missoula: Scholars Press, 1978).

5   Stimulating literary essays are difficult to find because they are scarce. The following selective list may be helpful. A justly famous characterization of Hebrew narrative is Eric Auerbach, "Odysseus' Scar", in his book, Mimesis (Princeton: Princeton University, 1953) 3-23. Similarly broad, but considerably different, perspectives may be found in Robert Alter, "A Literary Aproach to the Bible", Commentary 60/6 (December, 1975); "Biblical Type Scenes and the Uses of Convention", Critical Inquiry, Winter (1978)

355-68; "Biblical Narrative", Commentary 61/5 (May, 1976); also, Jacob Licht, Storytelling in the Bible (Jerusalem: Magnes Press, 1978). For individual essays on particular stories, see for example Charles Conroy, Absalom Absalom! Narrative and Language in 2 Sam 13-20 (Rome: Pontifical Biblical Institute, 1978); James L. Crenshaw, Samson: A Secret Betrayed, A Vow Ignored (Atlanta: John Knox, 1978); Kenneth R. R. Gros Louis, James S. Ackerman, Thayer S. Warshaw, eds., Literary Interpretations of Biblical Narratives (Nashville: Abingdon, 1974); Michael Fishbane, Text and Texture: Close Readings of Selected Biblical Texts (New York: Schocken Books, 1979); J. P. Fokkelman, Narrative Art in Genesis: Specimens of Stylistic and Structural Analysis (Assen/Amsterdam: Van Gorcum, 1975); David M. Gunn, The Story of King David: Genre and Interpretation (Sheffield: JSOT Press, 1978) and The Fate of King Saul: An Interpretation of a Biblical Story (Sheffield: JSOT Press, 1980); Jonathan Magonet, Form and Meaning: Studies in Literary Techniques in the Book of Jonah (Bern: Lang, 1976). See also recent issues of the journal, Semeia.

NOTES TO CHAPTER ONE

The Joseph Story: A Tale of Son and Father

1   Mircea Eliade, "Literary Imagination and Religious Structure", Criterion 17 (1978) 30-34; also his book, The Sacred and the Profane: The Nature of Religion (New York: Harcourt, Brace, 1959) 205.

For further reading on the Joseph story, see for example George W. Coats, From Canaan to Egypt: Structural and Theological Context for the Joseph Story (Washington: Catholic Biblical Association, 1976); Dorothy Irvin, "The Joseph and Moses Stories as Narrative in the Light of Ancient Near Eastern Narrative", in John H. Hayes and J. Maxwell Miller, eds., Israelite and Judaean History (Philadelphia: Westminster; London: SCM, 1977) 180-193; Donald B. Redford, A Study of the Biblical Story of Joseph (Leiden: Brill, 1970) chapter 4; Mary Savage, "A Rhetorical Analysis of the Joseph Narrative", in Carl D. Evans, William W. Hallo, John B. White, eds., Scripture in Context: Essays on the Comparative Method (Pittsburgh: Pickwick, 1980) 79-100;

James A. Seybold, "Paradox and Symmetry in the Joseph Narrative", in Kenneth R. R. Gros Louis, ed., Literary Interpretations of Biblical Narratives (Nashville: Abingdon, 1974) 59-73.

2   Northrop Frye, Fables of Identity: Studies in Poetic Mythology (New York: Harcourt, Brace, 1963) 19.

3   See Joseph Campbell, The Hero with a Thousand Faces (New York: Bollingen Foundation, 1949).

4   Victor Turner, The Ritual Process (Chicago: Aldine, 1969) chapters 3-5 (and see below, "Moses", p. 42). Note also Arnold van Gennep, Rites of Passages (Chicago: University of Chicago, 1960).

NOTES TO CHAPTER TWO

Wounded Beginnings: David and Two Sons

1   See Charles Conroy, Absalom Absalom! Narrative and Language in 2 Sam 13-20 (Rome: Pontifical Biblical Institute, 1978), a book which deepens the technical study of the King David materials by giving very close attention to details of language and style. Independently, we have come to share a number of perspectives on 2 Samuel 13. See also on this chapter, George Rideout, "The Rape of Tamar: A Rhetorical Analysis of 2 Samuel 13:1-22", in J. Jackson and M. Kessler, eds., Rhetorical Criticism (Pittsburgh: Pickwick, 1974) 75-84. For the story in a larger context: Kenneth R. R. Gros Louis, "The Difficulty of Ruling Well: King David of Israel", Semeia 8 (1977) 15-33; David M. Gunn, The Story of King David: Genre and Interpretation (Sheffield: JSOT Press, 1978) chapter 5; and compare Burke O. Long, "A Darkness Between Brothers: Solomon and Adonijah", Journal for the Study of the Old Testament 19 (1981) 79-94.

2   The feminine suffix can refer to the food (leḥem) or to Tamar.

3   Other instances of repetition as a stylistic device of Hebrew narratives have been discussed by Robert Alter, "Biblical Narrative", Commentary 61:5 (1976) 61-67, and Jacob Licht, Storytelling in the Bible (Jerusalem: Magnes

Press, 1978) 51-95.

4   The terms occur repeatedly in vv 1-2, 4-8, 10-12. See Rideout (note 1 above).

5   All the Greek versions in 13:21 add further explanation for David's inaction: "and he would not harm Amnon, for he loved him, since he was his first-born".

6   The Greek text at v 21 already had mentioned the idea of "first-born", and it adds at v 27 the phrase, "And Absalom prepared a feast like the feast of the king" (emphasis mine), again suggesting an emerging aura of royal position.

7   The text of vv 23-39 need not be viewed as particularly disturbed because of the repeated mention of Absalom's fleeing (vv 34, 37a, 38). The story interweaves two thematic foci: the mourning scene at court, and the flight of Absalom into the land of Geshur, just as 2 Samuel 15-18 juxtaposes events of Absalom's rebellion with David's departure from Jerusalem. One may outline the pattern of thematic alternation:
- (a)   Absalom's flight (v 34a^a)
- (b)   Public mourning at court (v 34a^b-36)
- (c)   Absalom's flight (v 37a)
- (d)   Public, constant mourning at court (v 37b)
- (e)   Absalom's flight (v 38)

A similar repetition to express simultaneous action may be seen in 1 Kings 20:16-21 and Gen 22:6, 7-8.

8   See now Gunn (note 1 above) 88-94.

10   Bernhard Anderson, "From Analysis to Synthesis: The Interpretation of Genesis 1-11", Journal of Biblical Literature 97 (1978) 23-39.

NOTES TO CHAPTER THREE

Moses

1   The phrase is borrowed from Northrop Frye, The Educated Imagination (Toronto: Canadian Broadcasting Corp., 1963) chapter 3.

For indebtedness relating to the essay as a whole, I owe a great deal to G. von Rad, Old Testament Theology

(New York: MacMillan, 1962, 1965), especially on the Mosaic office and the eventfulness of the Biblical word. On the plague-narrative and for general summaries of the scholarship on many points, my greatest debt is to Brevard S. Childs, The Book of Exodus: A Critical Theological Commentary (Philadelphia: Westminster; London: SCM, 1974). I also found very helpful J. Plastaras, The God of Exodus (Milwaukee: Bruce, 1966); also, on the character of Moses and his prophetic status, Martin Buber, Moses (New York: Harper and Row, 1958).

Some further literary approaches to the Moses materials: James S. Ackerman, "The Literary Context of the Moses Birth Story", and Hillel Barzel, "Moses: Tragedy and Sublimity", in K. R. R. Gros Louis, ed., Literary Interpretations of Biblical Narratives (Nashville: Abingdon, 1974) chapters 6 and 7; Michael Fishbane, "Exodus 1-4: The Prologue to the Exodus Cycle", in Text and Texture: Close Readings of Selected Biblical Texts (New York: Schocken Books, 1979) chapter 4; Moshe Greenberg, Understanding Exodus (New York: Behrman House Inc., for The Melton Research Center of the Jewish Theological Seminary of America, 1969); Charles D. Isbell, "The Structure of Exodus 1:1-14:31", and David M. Gunn, "Exodus 1-14: Plot, Character and Theology", in D. J. A. Clines, D. M. Gunn, A. J. Hauser, eds., Art and Meaning: Rhetoric in Biblical Literature (Sheffield: JSOT Press, 1981); David Robertson, "Comedy and Tragedy: Exodus 1-15 and the Bacchae", in The Old Testament and the Literary Critic (Philadelphia: Fortress, 1977) chapter 2.

2   See Giambattista Vico, The New Science (Ithaca: Cornell University, 1968).

3   For the concept of the Hebrew dissent from the state's "monopoly of force" I am indebted to George E. Mendenhall, The Tenth Generation: The Origins of the Biblical Tradition (Baltimore/London: Johns Hopkins, 1969).

4   See further Victor Turner, The Ritual Process: Structure and Anti-Structure (Chicago: University of Chicago, 1969) especially chapters 4-6.

5   For similar reflections on the beginning of narratives and their linking and continuation into sequels, see Larry D. Benson, Mallory's Morte d'Arthur (Cambridge, Mass.: Harvard University, 1977) 4-16.

6   On the concept of this uncleanness see Mary Douglas, Purity and Danger (Harmondsworth: Penguin, 1970) chapter 3.

NOTES TO CHAPTER FOUR

In Strange Ways: The Story of Samson

1   For other literary approaches to the Samson story, see now James L. Crenshaw, Samson: A Secret Betrayed, A Vow Ignored (Atlanta: John Knox, 1978); also J. Cheryl Exum, "Aspects of Symmetry and Balance in the Samson Saga", Journal for the Study of the Old Testament 19 (1981) 3-29.

2   Theodore Gaster, Myth, Legend, and Custom in the Old Testament (New York: Harper and Row, 1969) II, 433.

3   John L. McKenzie, The World of the Judges (Englewood Cliffs: Prentice-Hall, 1966) 158.

4   C. F. Burney, The Book of Judges (New York: KTAV, 1970 [first published 1918]) I, 342a.

NOTES TO CHAPTER FIVE

The Contest of Darius' Guards

1   For further reading see S. A. Cook, "I Esdras", in R. H. Charles, ed., The Apocrypha and Pseudepigrapha of the Old Testament (Oxford: Clarendon, 1913); Jacob M. Myers, I & II Esdras (Anchor Bible; Garden City, N.Y.: Doubleday, 1974) 44-57; C. C. Torrey, Ezra Studies (with introduction by W. F. Stinespring; New York: KTAV, 1970 [originally published 1910] 37-61.

2   I am indebted to William Goodman, Jr., for this interesting parallel ("A Study of 1 Esdras 3:1-5:6", Duke Ph.D. Dissertation, 1971, 210-211). Plays on words dictate the course of this argument: para poton and para pothon (drinking/arousing desire); stenonta and sthenonta (groaning/strong).

3   The text is given in Latin by R. Laqueur ("Ephoros. Die Proömium", Hermes 46 [1911] 172), who found it in Ludolf, Comentarius ad suam Historiam Aethiopicam (1681).

4   Other similar folktales may be found in Haim Schwarzbaum, Studies in Jewish and World Folklore (Berlin: de Gruyter, 1968) 319-21.

5   On the composition of the narrative and its relation to its "framework" see further, Frank Zimmerman, "The Story of the three Guardsmen", Jewish Quarterly Review 54 (1963/64) 179-200; he emphasizes the many incongruities within the present story and explains them as errors resulting from faulty translation from Aramaic into Greek, as well as from pious redaction; K.-F. Pöhlmann, Studien zum dritten Esra (Göttingen: Vandenhoeck & Ruprecht, 1970) 38-47; he also suggests a Semitic background for the dialogue; also William Goodman (note 2 above).

6   The same root that is used for facing a lion also describes man's gazing upon a beautiful woman (theorei/ theorousin).

7   Robert H. Pfeiffer (History of New Testament Times with an Introduction to the Apocrypha [New York: Harper and Row, 1949] 256) notes the progress in the argument from lower to higher. He writes that it begins by celebrating material and morally inferior wine, then proceeds to a higher level, the king. He also perceives humor, pathos, comedy, and tragedy in showing the "weaker" sex to be strongest. "Here he ranges...from the noblest (mother love and wifely devotion) to the lowest (selfish whims and silly fancies of coquettes bringing ruin to their lovers): even the king is helpless before a woman's wiles. But mightier than anything else is truth: magna est veritas, et praevalet! (4:41)".

8   Paul Humbert ("'Magna est veritas et praevalet' [3 Esra 4:35]", Orientalistische Literaturzeitung 31 [1928] 148-150) calls attention to striking affinities with Egyptian wisdom (Ptah-hotep ¶5 and The Tale of the Eloquent Peasant ¶92 and 95) and argues for a common saying throughout the ancient world. See James Pritchard, Ancient Near Eastern Texts Relating to the Old Testament (3rd edn., Princeton: Princeton University, 1969) 412-414, 407-410.

NOTES TO CHAPTER SIX

A Man Given Over to Trouble: The Story of King Saul

1   D. H. Lawrence, David (New York: Knopf, 1926); Adam Welch, "Saul", in Kings and Prophets of Israel (London: Lutterworth, 1952) 63-79.

2   For details of my indebtedness to, and disagreements with, other Biblical critics, see my book, The Fate of King Saul: An Interpretion of a Biblical Story (Sheffield: JSOT Press, 1980). The fuller treatment grew out of this essay written specifically for the present volume. In the book I explore further the key scenes of rejection (1 Samuel 13 and 15), the interplay of Saul and David, some of the more striking imagery in the writing, the tragic dimension, and the role of God. For further reading: Peter R. Ackroyd, The First Book of Samuel (Cambridge Bible Commentary on the New English Bible; Cambridge: C.U.P., 1971); W. G. Blaikie, The First Book of Samuel (The Expositor's Bible; London: Hodder and Stoughton, 1888); James Hastings, "Saul", "Jonathan", "David", in The Greater Men and Women of the Bible (London: T.&T.Clark, 1914) 63-160; H. W. Hertzberg, I & II Samuel: A Commentary (London: SCM; Philadelphia: Westminster, 1964); W. Lee Humphreys, "The Tragedy of King Saul: A Study of the Structure of I Samuel 9-31", Journal for the Study of the Old Testament 6 (1978) 18-27; David Jobling, "Jonathan: A Structural Study in 1 Samuel", in The Sense of Biblical Narrative (Sheffield: JSOT Press, 1978) 4-25 - a fine study of Jonathan as mediator between Saul and David.

3   The "family" dimension to the story is also prominent in the account of King David, 2 Samuel and 1 Kings 1-2. See Chapter Two in this volume: "Wounded Beginnings: David and Two Sons".

INDEX OF BIBLICAL PASSAGES

INDEX OF BIBLICAL NAMES